HOW TO PRAY FOR YOUR UNBEL...

Also by Michael Fanstone:
  The Sheep That Got Away (1992)
  Together Apart (1994)

How To Pray For Your Unbelieving Husband

MICHAEL AND DIANE FANSTONE

MONARCH

Crowborough

British Library Cataloguing Data
A catalogue record for this book is available
from the British Library.

ISBN 1 85424 378 0

Designed and produced by Bookprint Creative Services
P.O. Box 827, BN21 3YJ, England for
MONARCH PUBLICATIONS
Broadway House, The Broadway,
Crowborough, East Sussex, TN6 1HQ.
Printed in Great Britain.

Introduction

While being married can and should be a pleasurable and fulfilling experience, if you are in a relationship as a Christian with someone who does not share your faith, it can lead to tensions you could do without.

First of all, we want you to know that we have written this book because we understand something of these stresses. We recognise that life may be difficult and demanding for you at home, at least some of the time. This is not surprising if you and your spouse have different perspectives on something that is central to your life.

One of the reasons we have compiled this book is because we want you to be encouraged. We do not have any quick fix solutions. What we can do, however, is to point you each day towards the God who will walk with you through everything you encounter.

It would be wonderful for us all if we could assure you that if you did this and prayed that, your husband would turn to Jesus Christ and all your problems would be solved. In practice, while we have no hesitation at all in assuring you that God will invest his resources to help that happen, it will also take an open mind and a willingness to change on the part of your husband before that great day comes.

There are sufficient devotions in the following pages to provide you with a different reading and meditation for about four months. Our goal overall has been to point you to God, encourage you to trust him, and to suggest to you that there may be positive things you can do or pray which could help your husband come to Christ. We suspect strongly that God has a part for you to play in the plans he has for your home.

We want to suggest that you pray each day on the theme of that day's meditation. To help you get started we have included the first sentence or two. After this comes either a question which we encourage you to answer, or a practical task you could undertake. In either case, we want to leave you with something relevant to think about or do during the day.

We recognise that everyone's circumstances are different and that the material some days will be more relevant for you than on others. However, our prayer is that God will meet you, speak to you and help you in a variety of ways as you use these devotions. Please write and tell us, via our publisher, if your life changes as you read and use this book.

Michael and Diane Fanstone
Gravesend, 1997

Acknowledgements

We are very grateful to those who have helped us by reading and assessing the early drafts of our material. Sylvia Austen, Jenny Miller, Marion Sherwood and Marion Thompson have all made numerous suggestions which have resulted in the final text being much clearer and easier to read. However, we accept full responsibility for anything insensitive or unhelpful.

Will He? Won't He?

Let us run with perseverance... (Hebrews 12:1)

Read: Hebrews 11:32-12:3

It was Monday morning and Rosemary was despondent. Just three months earlier her husband, James, had willingly gone to a church social event with her and, when they got back into the car to go home afterwards, had said how much he had enjoyed it. What pleased Rosemary was the relaxed way he had talked to so many of her church friends even though he had not met most of them before. Since then he had even been to church services once or twice, and seemed to be thinking seriously about the Christian faith.

However, on this particular Sunday morning and for no obvious reason, James told Rosemary the bad news. He said that he would not come to church today, and doubted he would ever go again. Despite all her probing he would not tell her why, and to this day Rosemary still does not understand what prompted his dramatic change of attitude.

Your spouse may be changeable too. One moment you feel he is so near to committing his life to Jesus Christ; the next he seems to be a million miles away. Maybe you have prayed for him for years, and you keep having your hopes raised and then dashed because his reaction to Christianity seems to alter more than the weather.

God's Word encourages us not to be too discouraged by this. Whatever happens at home, keep your eyes on Jesus and trust him to keep on working quietly in your partner's life. God honours persevering faith.

A Prayer I confess I struggle when my husband's response to you changes for no apparent reason. Please increase my faith so that I can trust you to keep working in his life whether I see any obvious signs of response or not.

A Practical Suggestion In order to try to maintain some Christian contact, see if you can arrange a time when you and your husband can meet socially with a couple he already knows and likes from your church.

The Pain of Being Misunderstood

No wound was found on him, because he had trusted in his God (Daniel 6:23)

Read: Daniel 6:1-23

Having your motives questioned and loyalty doubted is painful – as Joanna found out. She first discovered how real God's love for her was when she visited a women's morning group at her local church while her children were at school. She became a Christian after just a few visits, but found that her husband became uncharacteristically antagonistic as soon as she told him about it. This perplexed Joanna, whose dream was to love and be loved by both God and her husband at the same time.

Daniel in our Bible reading had the same problem. He was wholly dedicated to serving King Darius but, when it came to a blunt choice, Daniel knew that he had to put God first. As he continued praying regularly to God, he knew that he might be penalised severely.

Your dedication to God may also be misunderstood as your family interprets your faith as a threat. They may think that you have religious mania and care less about them than you used to. Of course, you know this is untrue, and that your love towards them and commitment to them is not threatened at all by your love for God and desire to serve him.

God took good care of Daniel, but he had to spend the night with some hungry lions whose mouths God miraculously kept tightly closed. When others misunderstand you as they did Daniel, remember that God knows your heart and motives and will support you too – however he does it.

A Prayer I want to keep close to you, Lord, but also want to know if I am unnecessarily antagonising members of my family by being insensitive or too preoccupied with Christian activities. Help me to be loyal to both you and them – even if they do not see it that way.

A Practical Suggestion If some people you live or work with seem to misunderstand your faith, check whether there is something positive you can do to help build stronger relationships with them.

The Protective Hand of God

The Lord was with Joseph and he prospered... (Genesis 39:2)

Read: Genesis 37:12-28

One morning, when Tim had left for work, Jemma sat alone in the lounge feeling miserable. Even when her husband was there, the communication between them was poor and the affection minimal. Sadly, he changed the night Jemma came home and told him with great excitement that she had become a Christian. Until then, she had no idea that he had an aversion to any kind of religious faith, but now she feels isolated from the man she loves.

Joseph felt incredibly alone as his brothers sold him to Midianite merchants who took him prisoner to Egypt where he was traded once again. At a stroke, he was ruthlessly separated from his entire family, and he must have especially missed his doting father's love and attention (37:3). The pain of separation was undoubtedly intense.

Other wives know this pain too. One has said, 'My becoming a Christian has meant leading separate lives, with different values and differing sources of enjoyment.' Another agreed, saying, 'I feel lonely and isolated because my husband has no concept of a spiritual life.'

God completely understood how Joseph felt and stayed close to him, gradually putting in place his plans for Joseph's future. Despite times when both Jemma and you feel humanly isolated, God is doing the same for you. He has already mapped out his future direction for your life. His invitation to you today is to trust him.

A Prayer Please reassure me today, Lord, that you are with me now and always will be – whatever happens. Let me sense your fatherly support and encouragement.

A Practical Suggestion To help your husband know how much you still love him, ask him what he would like to do the next time you can share leisure time together. Then go along with him and enjoy his choice – even if you detest fishing!

Learning to Forgive

Do not let the sun go down while you are still angry (Ephesians 4:26)

Read: Ephesians 4:17-27

Jane never anticipated the effect her new-found faith would have on her husband, Rob. From the moment she first told him of her response to Christ's love, he became angry and, while he remained fairly easy-going on the surface, he often seemed irritable, and tended to criticise her with very little provocation. Try as she might, she could never find out why he was behaving like this towards her, and so she felt powerless to help heal the gaping wound that was developing in their relationship.

Jane knew from the teaching in her church how crucial it is for Christians not to hold on to resentment and bitter feelings, or to let relationship problems fester by allowing unresolved tensions to remain unattended. Whenever she could, in any area of life, Jane faced problems head-on so that she could sleep with a clear conscience. Ironically, it was a problem she faced at home that seemed to her impossible to get to grips with.

Coping with an on-going difficulty like Jane's is demanding and draining because, apart from other reactions, she felt guilty at her inability to put things right. For now, at least, this seemed to be impossible as Rob would not discuss it. Writing to the Ephesian Christians, Paul tells them how, as Christ's disciples, they must 'speak truthfully' (v25) and make genuine attempts to restore relationships when they can. If Jane retains this as her goal, she will undoubtedly know the continuing support of God.

A Prayer Please help me to remain committed to restoring any relationship in my life that is strained, Lord, however long it takes. I want all the relationships in my life to please you.

A Question to Answer Have you tried to understand why there are difficulties in any of your relationships? Try thinking the whole situation through in detail from the other person's perspective. Ask God for his unique insight.

A Gift to the Lord

So now I give him to the Lord (1 Samuel 1:28)

Read: 1 Samuel 1:21-28

It was Emma's thirteenth birthday, and Noreen and Don tried to make it a special morning for their daughter before she left for school. This year they found themselves able to give her a more expensive present than usual, and were delighted that she was so happy when she opened it. Later, when everyone else had left the house, Noreen was praying specifically for Emma when God spoke to her, showing her that the most important gift she could ever give her daughter was her prayers. She sensed strongly that these should be regular, specific, and cover all aspects of her life and future. If she was unaware of it before, Noreen now knew clearly that, as a Christian wife and mother, she had a responsibility to pray regularly for her family.

When Samuel was born, Hannah had no doubt that God had deliberately intervened and answered her prayers (1 Sam 1:11). He was still very young when she dedicated him to God's service. She did so, not only because she had made a binding promise, but because she had a deep confidence in God. If Samuel lived according to God's divine plan as he grew up, then his life would be fulfilling as well as bringing glory to God.

God spoke very specifically to Noreen about praying to God regularly for her children. In her case, with Don not having become a Christian yet, this was even more important. To be honest, it is the most responsible thing any Christian parent can ever do for their child.

A Prayer Having prayed for my husband and children today, Lord, please help me to follow Hannah's example and not to snatch them back as if their spiritual future is my responsibility. I entrust them to you and know that you will take very good care of them.

A Practical Suggestion Make a prayer journal for each day so that you pray regularly for your children. Remember their schooling, friendships, relationships, protection in teenage years, conversion to Christ, spiritual growth, their future partners and maybe even your grandchildren.

Belonging Together

Though all its parts are many, they form one body (1 Corinthians 12:12)

Read: 1 Corinthians 12:1-14

Things were not right and Janice knew it. Going to church proved to be a difficult experience because she found that she did not talk to many people. Janice knew she was not the most vivacious person around, but nor was she shy and withdrawn. She also knew what the problem was.

Janice was only able to get to church on Sundays occasionally because her husband kept arranging to go out or to see friends. This meant that it became harder and harder to go because she felt increasingly like an outsider. The church held a mid-week daytime housegroup but Janice never went to this either, although she could have done. She felt isolated from the people, and embarrassed that she hardly ever attended on Sundays. Janice does not need anyone to tell her that her next decision will probably be to disassociate herself from the church altogether.

When Paul wrote 1 Corinthians 12 to the Christians in Corinth, he could not emphasise enough how much all Christians belong together and need each other. For him, mutual fellowship, along with using the varied spiritual gifts God gives to every Christian, was not of secondary importance. On the contrary, he believed staunchly that Christianity which ignores the corporate element is hardly recognisable as Christianity at all. If, like Janice, your involvement at church is limited and your relationships shallow, try not to give up. The reality is that you need these other Christians, and they need you!

A Prayer Help me to grasp the importance you place on Christians relating closely together as your family on earth. If I am ever in danger of becoming isolated, please alert me.

A Practical Suggestion List all the times you can remember that another Christian has taught, encouraged or helped you in any way. Then thank God for those members of his family who have contributed to your Christian life.

When Things Go Sour...

They had such a sharp disagreement... (Acts 15:39)

Read: Acts 15:36-41

Margaret and her husband have been married for some years. They generally get on well, but the issue of Margaret's faith, and her desire to meet with other Christians, is virtually guaranteed to cause disruption to their household. On many occasions she has to compromise by missing meetings at church because she fears a row at home if she says she is going. It is a situation to which she has grown accustomed after so long, although it makes her sad.

In 2 Corinthians 6:14-18 we see why a home a Christian shares with an unbeliever is almost certain to be caught up in conflict sometimes. Even the Apostle Paul and his close friend and colleague, Barnabas, fell out over whether or not they should take John Mark on a missionary trip. Having deserted them once before, Paul felt Mark was a liability, while Barnabas sensed he should be given a second chance. For some reason they were completely unable to resolve their disagreement, and split up.

Does this mean that situations like Margaret's are hopeless and that she should anticipate having to cope with the same problems for the rest of her life? In Philemon verse 24 Paul encourages John Mark by calling him his 'fellow-worker'. With God's help on a later occasion, Paul began to see John Mark in a different light and they were reconciled. God can work in any number of possible ways to help Margaret. She must ask him.

A Prayer Please help me to trust you, Lord, when we experience conflict at home because I want to be faithful to you. Please support me, and help me to be particularly sensitive and conciliatory when I can.

A Practical Suggestion Cook your husband one of his favourite dishes for dinner tonight.

Living God's Way

Live a life of love... (Ephesians 5:2)

Read: Ephesians 4:29-5:7

Rachel had taken her children to the park and, from a distance, she stood watching them play on the roundabout before going on to the swings and, later, the slide. They never seemed to get tired, and most of the time they were in the thick of the action. At times shivers went down Rachel's spine as she saw them hanging on precariously as others pushed the roundabout ever faster. Once, she even closed her eyes rather than see what would happen next!

As she reflected, Rachel realised that she had a tendency to act at home like her children did in the park. Ronnie, her husband, was not a practising Christian like her but, because Rachel's personal faith meant so much to her, she never tired of finding different ways to keep telling him how he needed to believe in Jesus Christ too. As she watched the children playing, she realised how precariously close she must get to putting him off Christianity for good.

Paul's encouragement to the Ephesian Christians was to live out their faith, and he draws attention to the example of Jesus who 'gave himself as a fragrant offering and sacrifice'. Ultimately, it was what Jesus did that paid the price for mankind's sin, not what he said. Ronnie is more likely to respond to her faith if, as a dedicated Christian wife, Rachel concentrates more on living it out in practice rather than continually haranguing him verbally. There is great power in the witness of a loving life.

A Prayer Please help me, Lord, to get to know you better – not so much in terms of head knowledge, but in a personal and intimate way, so that I can imitate you more, especially at home.

A Question to Answer Are there any particular things that you tend to do or say, regularly, which create barriers between you and your husband, making it harder for him to relate to the gospel? Try to avoid them.

Having Mutual Respect

Bear with each other... (Colossians 3:13)

Read: Colossians 3:1-17

Both Valerie and John attended church when they married but, as the years went by, he found other things to do on Sundays, and preferred to stay at home while she went alone. This led to an increasing difficulty, for while John became less and less interested in spiritual issues, Valerie found that her faith was growing, and that God was becoming more important to her. At the same time, problems at home got worse whenever they tried to discuss issues of significance.

One day it dawned on Valerie how much she disliked and even resented John. The more she thought about it, the more she became worried as to where it could lead. Wisely, she decided to talk to her church's female pastoral worker who showed her that, as far as possible, she needed to understand, love and respect her husband – despite their different priorities. She reminded Valerie that one of the great strengths of Christianity is that, with God's help, Christians can display a tolerance and acceptance of those who, humanly, irritate and aggravate them. Jesus' love can be so powerful a resource that they can even respond with dignity and respect – as Jesus did when he was confronted and opposed.

If there is one thing that eventually may bring John to Jesus Christ, it will be Valerie's respect and love for him – especially when he deserves it least. However, in the meantime, Valerie has to be prepared to be patient and faithful for as long as it takes.

A Prayer Although I sometimes find it hard to be tolerant, Lord, help me today to appreciate the good things about my husband, and to respect his views – even if I cannot agree with them. Help me to become more like Jesus, I ask.

A Question to Answer If Jesus lived in your house, how do you think he would handle the way your husband feels about him and the church?

The Annoying Tap!

A quarrelsome wife is like a constant dripping (Proverbs 19:13)

Read: Proverbs 19:1-14

No one doubted Julie's motives, least of all Kevin, but he was left in no doubt at all that her faith was not for him. When she first told him that she wanted to go to church, he found it amusing. He reacted with characteristic caution but did not stand in her way. Once she became a Christian and wanted to spend more time with her church friends, however, he started to become slightly irritated. Kevin really stopped seeing the funny side of it when Julie began to pressurise him into going to church too. He had made up his mind long before that religion was not for him, and Julie's pestering began to drive a wedge between them, especially as every day she tried to change his mind. Their marriage was falling apart at the seams.

The often-ignored Bible book of Proverbs is full of God's revealed wisdom on how to live in God's way. In today's verse, wives are reminded that relentless arguing or nagging tends to have the same irritating qualities as the tap in the kitchen sink that drips when a new washer is needed. However well-intentioned she may be, a Christian wife is more likely to see her husband show interest in her faith if she witnesses constantly by her life, occasionally by her words, and prays regularly for God's revelation to break through to his heart and mind.

A Prayer Please, Lord, give me wisdom to control my enthusiasm for you, by being very careful what I do and say in front of close members of my family who do not know you yet. May my life shine for you and my prayers for them be answered.

A Practical Suggestion Make a point of listening carefully to yourself during an hour spent with your husband. Then try to put yourself in his shoes and evaluate the way you behaved and the words you spoke. Try to assess whether you helped to draw him closer to yourself as his wife and to God's kingdom or whether you pushed him further away.

God is Fair with Everyone

There is no favouritism with him (Ephesians 6:9)

Read: Ephesians 6:5-9

'I just don't understand', Jean said to Hazel in a puzzled voice. 'I've been a Christian for almost eight years and I've done everything I know to get Roger to become a Christian, but he still isn't the least bit interested. He only comes to church at Christmas because I threaten to rebel when his parents visit if he doesn't. Janet has only been a Christian for eighteen months, yet she told me yesterday that her husband responded to the appeal on Sunday and became a Christian. He only began coming to church a month ago. I really don't think it's fair. Why doesn't God answer my prayers?'

We can see why Jean feels upset, hurt, bewildered and possibly angry. It looks as if God has overlooked her while showing special favour to Janet. The Psalmist feels the same way in Psalm 44:23-24. It is at times like this, though, that we need to look more deeply at the underlying issues.

Today's passage includes Paul's teaching to masters and slaves, two very different groups of people. The lifestyle of each was a million miles from the other, and yet, when God views them, he sees an equality that human beings cannot easily detect. God does not favour Janet over Jean, nor one husband above the other. He wants both of them in his Kingdom and will keep sending his Holy Spirit to reveal more spiritual truth to Roger so that in due course, when he is ready, he can make his own personal response to Jesus too.

A Prayer Lord, please help me not to get resentful when other people's prayers seem to get answered sooner than mine. Rather, encourage me to keep praying with even more passion for those who have not yet responded to your love.

A Question to Answer What answers to your prayers has God given you in the past?

God's Reluctant Missionaries

Jonah was greatly displeased and became angry (Jonah 4:1)

Read: Jonah 4:1-11

Within months of their wedding, Jean started to wonder if she should ever have married Stuart. Having become a Christian at fifteen, she had seen some of her school friends commit their lives to Jesus too so, when she met Stuart and they fell in love, she presumed the same would happen to him. All he needed was time. Yet as their relationship increased in intensity, she knew that he was not coming any closer to God at all. What affected Jean most was the way that Stuart began to use offensive and blasphemous language once they were married. After that, sensing he would never become a Christian, she stopped trying to tell him about Jesus, and did her best to keep her church friends away from her home because she expected Stuart to embarrass her. Nor did she want him to come to church with her; it was easier to keep the two areas of life apart.

Jonah had no desire at all to see God work in the lives of the Ninevites. To be honest, he detested them and thought that they deserved God's harshest judgement, not his most generous mercy. Right to the end of this Bible book Jonah remained angry at the way God had worked through him.

The transforming miracle that God worked in the lives of the people of Ninevah shows the enormousness of his power and love. You may be a reluctant missionary like Jonah, but God can surprise you too if you remain obedient to him.

A Prayer Like Jonah, I find it very easy to look at my situation through human eyes alone. Please give me a clear understanding of what you could accomplish through my life, and then fill me with your Holy Spirit so that it can happen.

A Practical Suggestion Head for your local Christian bookshop and find a biography to take home to read. Choose one which tells how God has worked significantly in and through someone who had offered their life to him. Be encouraged by it!

Reflecting on Priorities

Don't you care that my sister has left me to do the work...? (Luke 10:40)

Read: Luke 10:38-42

When he arrived home from work, Bruce always seemed to find Gilly at the table poring over the Bible and a pile of study books, and it was a source of considerable aggravation to him. In reality, of course, it was only once or twice a week that it happened, but it meant on these occasions that, despite a busy and demanding day at work, he had to wait for maybe over an hour for his dinner. He felt that this was unreasonable.

For him, this raised the whole question of Gilly's priorities. Gilly was not trying to be difficult, but she did tend to get carried away and did not know when to stop. Bruce saw it as a sign that her faith was much more important to her than he was and he resented it.

Martha was unhappy too, when Mary sat listening to Jesus while she slaved over a hot stove. She thought it was unfair and unreasonable, and appealed to Jesus for support. She must have been surprised to hear him commend Mary. He did so on that occasion because, being with them for such a short time, he knew that his spiritual food was more important than the food which Martha was worrying about.

Our task is to get our priorities right too – not an easy thing to do. Usually we have to balance our many responsibilities against each other but, in view of Jesus' words, we need to make sure we neither ignore him nor the food!

A Prayer I struggle so often, Lord, when trying to assess what ought to be my priorities at any given time. Please guide me so that I neither compromise my faith by giving you too little time and attention, nor my husband by apparently communicating to him that he does not matter much to me.

A Question to Answer Think through carefully and in detail the impression you gave your husband yesterday. Did your actions, attitudes and words tell him that he is, for you, the most important person in the world?

19

Keeping Secrets

She sent word to the rulers of the Philistines (Judges 16:18)

Read: Judges 16:1-21

Margaret really enjoyed attending the group run by her church for women whose husbands did not yet believe in Jesus. The most valuable part was finding that others understood exactly how she felt. At home, life was not easy for her. Her husband had been made redundant by his firm, and was angry and resentful. Also, he did not appreciate Margaret's faith and the time she spent at church. The consequence was that when Margaret was safely surrounded by her friends, she tended to talk very freely and openly about Bill. Indeed, sometimes her friends squirmed uncomfortably as she described things that happened at home. Eventually, the pastor's wife took Margaret aside and suggested kindly that she was more discreet about how much she divulged to the group in future.

Wherever the dividing line is between what is confidential within a relationship and what can be shared outside of it, Delilah was clearly the wrong side of it. Her sole intention was to betray Samson once he divulged the secret of his strength. Sadly, when he could stand her nagging no longer and told her the truth, she revealed it to the Philistines, who took immediate advantage of him. Despite his love for her, Delilah had no sense of loyalty to him at all.

Proverbs 2:6 tells us that 'the Lord gives wisdom'. How valuable this special gift is when we need the discretion to know when it is best to speak and when it is best to keep quiet.

A Prayer Recognising, Lord, that I often feel torn between different people to whom I have a sense of responsibility, I ask for your wisdom so that I say the right things. Please save me from making a habit of saying the wrong thing in the wrong place at the wrong time – but forgive me when I do.

A Practical Suggestion If, like Margaret, you are in a position where you can easily slip into divulging what should be confidential between you and your husband, work out carefully now how much you feel comfortable about telling your friends at church during the course of conversation. Then do not overstep the mark.

He Listens

The Lord remembered her (1 Samuel 1:19)

Read: 1 Samuel 1:1-20

Carol knew only too well what the pastor was talking about when, in his Sunday sermon, he spoke of the need for Christians to pray relentlessly. She, and some of her friends, had been praying for a very long time for her husband, Frank, to become a Christian, but so far the most encouraging thing to have happened was that, one Christmas, he went to church for a carol service. Even that was three years ago, and there were times when Carol seriously considered stopping praying for him. She found the continual disappointment hard to cope with.

Hannah's experience is a source of great encouragement to any praying women carrying a heavy burden. God hears all our prayers but, for reasons best known to him, he keeps some of us waiting a long time for a definitive reply. It would suit us better to hear straight back from God, but sometimes his 'wait' signal means that he wants to teach us patience and perseverance as we continue to pray.

Eventually Hannah's prayer was answered and she gave birth to a son, Samuel. Carol knows that this by no means guarantees her the answer she longs for, but the mere fact that God still listens after years and years of praying the same prayer is a source of great encouragement to her.

A Prayer I am aware, Lord, that being human I want what I pray for right now. Despite my impatience, help me to keep praying so that my faith in you grows through this experience of waiting. Then, Lord, when you do start to speak to my husband, please help him to be ready to respond to you.

A Practical Suggestion Let God know how serious you are. Why not tell him that your husband's conversion is so important to you that you promise him you will pray every day until your husband comes to faith?

It's Hard to Believe

Sarah laughed to herself (Genesis 18:12)

Read: Genesis 18:1-15

Elizabeth had managed to get to her housegroup this week, but it was something that happened only comparatively rarely. As the Bible study progressed, she found herself struggling with the message. When she married Greg she had done so against the advice of her friends at church. He was slightly interested in her faith, but was still a long way from making a personal commitment. Her goal had been to see him converted but, instead, as the years had gone by, he had slipped further away from God, and now she despaired of him ever coming to him. It was precisely this that caused her pain in the housegroup because, as they were discussing possible miracles, her friend Virginia had asked her pointedly, 'Wouldn't it be fantastic if Greg became a Christian this year?' Inside, Elizabeth laughed. She knew it could not happen. She lived with Greg, and she knew him only too well.

Sarah in this Bible passage had thought it equally bizarre when she heard the prediction that she would bear a child at the age of ninety. She perceived it to be totally impossible, but she had not taken into account the kind of miracles God can do. Nor had Elizabeth, but she did sense that for Greg to become a Christian was well beyond what she could believe in at present.

What Elizabeth had not realised is that God's power is unlimited although, of course, before anyone can become a Christian, that person needs to be open to revelation from God. Who knows what God may do next?

A Prayer Thank you, Lord, that despite Sarah's inability to believe, you gave her a son at the age of ninety. Please work out your plans for my family and me, even if my faith is somewhat smaller than I would like.

A Practical Suggestion Make a list of all the things you have ever heard that God has done for people you know. Then thank him.

A New Creation

If anyone is in Christ, there is a new creation (2 Corinthians 5:17)

Read: Galatians 5:13-26

Claire had been a Christian for six months. She had become a Christian through the quiet witness of her best friend, Sue. While having a coffee together one morning, Claire asked how she could be that same quiet witness to her husband, Joe, that Sue had been to her. Claire said that it was not so much what Sue had said, but the life she lived, that had made an impact on her. Sue suggested that Claire should read Galatians 5:22 which talks about the Fruit of the Spirit: love, joy, peace, patience, kindness, goodness, faithfulness, gentleness and self control.

As she read, Claire could also see what the Bible reveals in the preceding verses (5:19-21), about the sort of life lived by many who do not yet believe. She realised afresh that once someone becomes a Christian there is a new creation, and God begins to work deeply in their life. At this point a new person begins to emerge.

Claire needs to develop her relationship with Jesus by spending time getting to know him better. We do too. Then, gradually, but definitely, the Fruit of the Spirit will begin to become part of our lives and people will see that we are different. That in itself will be a witness to the Lord, and could well be the means by which other people, and especially those with whom we live, will see the reality and relevance of the Christian faith.

A Prayer Thank you, Lord, for all those Christians whose quiet witness has inspired and encouraged me. Help me to develop my relationship with you so that others will see you in me.

A Question to Answer Will you promise God that you will spend some time quietly each day seeking to deepen your relationship with him, so that his Fruit may begin to become part of your life?

Presence Assured

The Lord is with you when you are with him (2 Chronicles 15:2)

Read: 2 Chronicles 14:2-15:4

When she was single, Georgina did not realise the importance of the Christian fellowship and spiritual teaching she received through her church's youth group. Now, though, Georgina was in her early thirties, married with two young children, and what with her marital and parental responsibilities and part-time job, she had plenty to do. She was aware she had had no contact with Christians since she moved to her new home, but thought she could manage spiritually as things were, maybe getting back into a church when the children were older.

The last thing Georgina expected in her life was tragedy, but a phone call one morning brought news that her father had died of a sudden heart attack. Her life crumbled and she felt desperately lonely and sad, as one of the secure foundations in her life had been ripped away from under her.

It was then that thoughts of God flooded her mind. She recalled her previously close relationship with him and remembered how, whenever she drew close to him, he had come close to her. As Georgina cried to God, repented for ignoring him for so long, and turned back to him, he started, slowly at first, to become more real to her. The same thing happened as in the days of Asa when God responded so warmly to the sincere cries for help from his people. Georgina's grieving was still long and painful, but she knew God was supporting her. Even her husband was surprised at how she coped. Now God could begin to reach out to him…

A Prayer As I cry to you for help today, recognising how far I have strayed from you, please receive me back, Lord.

A Question to Answer Compared to the closest you have ever sensed you were to God, where are you today?

Living in Christ

Just as you received Christ Jesus as Lord, continue to live in him
(Colossians 2:6)

Read: Colossians 2:6-15

Jason did not feel he was disparaging about Ruth's faith but, ever since they had married nine months earlier, she felt he spoke disapprovingly about her church involvement. She knew he did not understand it; that was obvious from the talks they had with John, her minister, before their wedding. He had picked up traces of cynicism about Christianity in Jason, and had gently warned Ruth about it, but up until their wedding she had detected nothing. Now, just months later, she knew that John was right; Jason had some kind of resentment about Christianity and gradually seemed to be releasing it into their marriage. Ruth was seriously worried, but was delighted on a particular Sunday that she managed to get to church when John preached from Paul's letter to the Colossian Christians.

He then told the congregation that having opened their lives to receive Jesus Christ as Saviour and Lord, when the difficult and demanding times came along, as they surely would, sometimes they would be tempted to jettison their commitment to Christ. John continued by saying that to do so would be to deny the wonderful work of love and grace God had already accomplished. Indeed, it is when times are hard that God can work deeply in Christians' lives, and rooting and strengthening takes place.

Having been on the verge of giving up, Ruth went home more determined than ever to stay close to God, and to get to the bottom of Jason's resentment. Only then, with God's help, could they deal with it together.

A Prayer Thank you that you understand when I feel I have had enough, Lord. Thank you, too, for your renewed strength and vision to carry on when I need it most.

A Question to Answer Can you imagine how God would feel if you decided to stop loving and serving him? Try to think it through from his angle.

25

The Secondary Decisions

I will pay back four times the amount (Luke 19:8)

Read: Luke 19:1-10

As Katie met her fellow Christian mums at the school gate one morning they knew something had happened. Her face was radiant. Katie's husband, Jeremy, had committed his life to Jesus Christ the night before, and Katie was sure that it meant an end to all the family's recent problems. Within a couple of weeks, however, Katie's friends noticed that the glow was fading, and she was sounding worried. They discussed the situation and discovered that she was disappointed and in danger of becoming disillusioned. She had expected all the disagreements at home to end once Jeremy became a Christian, but, on recent occasions, they had been as bad as ever.

The transformation of Zacchaeus, who had a life-changing encounter with Jesus, shows us why. Not only did he have to repent of his past sin and put his trust in Jesus for the first time, but also, with God's help, he had to change his way of life. Zacchaeus began at once. No longer was he going to be a money-hungry thief; he would be fair, just and responsible. To show how different he would be, he made amends for all that he had dishonestly gained in the past. His new life in Christ showed through quickly!

For most new Christians the process of changing their lifestyle to become more like Jesus takes a long time. It gradually goes on from the moment of conversion until death. The best thing for Katie is not to expect too much too soon. The great news is that for Jeremy, the process has begun!

A Prayer Please help me to be patient, Lord, whenever I meet a new Christian. Help me to recall how definitely, yet sometimes slowly, the life-changing power of Jesus has affected my own life.

A Practical Suggestion Pick just one of the qualities of Jesus you know that you lack thus far in your life, then pray for it and ask God to help it develop in you – starting today.

What God Knows

You know me (Psalm 139:1)

Read: Psalm 139:1-18

Freda used to worry that her husband, John, knew very little about God. Furthermore, he seemed to have no desire to discover what Freda had experienced of God's love and care in the many years she had been a Christian. What increased Freda's sense of pain was that John would not discuss spiritual issues, which meant that she had no idea of what he was thinking. For many years she had had to live with this area of his life being a complete and total mystery. Overall, their marriage was good, but Freda really wanted to know how he felt about God.

Then one morning in her Bible reading she discovered Psalm 139. God spoke clearly to her through it, and reminded her that not only does he know everything about her, but he is also fully conversant with every aspect of John's life too. God made John and he knew him before he was born. He knows every movement in John's life. He knows his thoughts and is even aware of the words that will come out of John's mouth before anyone hears them.

These truths are now real to Freda, and she no longer worries that God has no interest in John. Because of this, she can pray more confidently that John will come to God through faith in Jesus. Even if John seems to have no interest in God, God is clearly interested in him. Even more remarkable is the truth that God has intimate knowledge of the life of every human being on earth – and that includes you and your husband too.

A Prayer Please help me to pray for my husband too, Lord. Thank you that you know all about him, and love him even more than I do.

A Practical Suggestion Read through these verses slowly and meditate on them again. Try to take in these amazing truths about God's knowledge of us.

Doing It God's Way

Let all the other men go (Judges 7:7)

Read: Judges 7:1-22

Judy was quite skilled at practical jobs around the home. When a wardrobe needed building, when the kitchen required replumbing or the lawn mower wanted repairing, Judy, armed with her toolbox, came to the rescue. Toby, her husband, left her to get on with many of the jobs, even though he was quite a handyman himself. It was just that Judy had a capacity to work out what was causing a problem, calculate the best way to rectify it, and then set to work to get it done. Only rarely did she not succeed.

She used this same gift with other problems too. She was helpful when friends had relationship problems, and when it came to how Toby would become a Christian, Judy had it all worked out. She assessed how much exposure he would need to the Gospel, how many contacts he would need with committed Christians, and worked out that in another two years or so at the mission her church was already beginning to plan, Toby would walk to the front and dedicate his life to Jesus Christ.

In reality, Judy's plans were as humanistic as Gideon's. God needed to teach Gideon a vital lesson the night the Israelites defeated the Midianites. Gideon had to learn that divine plans are often a million miles away from their human equivalent. What is more, they work much better. Judy needed to learn this too – and quickly, before she concluded that God had let her down. Her best course of action was to wait quietly for God to show his right way forward.

A Prayer Forgive me please, Lord, when I try to do your job for you – and make things harder for you as a result. It is so good to know you have things under control.

A Question to Answer Can you think of occasions in the past when you have come to your own conclusions as to how God would work, only to be taken aback when he has done things in a different way? Repent if you need to, but take time to rejoice that God is so good.

Viewing Things God's Way

No longer two, but one (Matthew 19:6)

Read: Matthew 19:1-12

Delia was at the end of her tether. Life at home was virtually intolerable. While she believed that her husband, Jamie, was the main problem because he worked all hours, she also knew that she had become increasingly intolerant and critical. Now that the children were on the verge of leaving home, she could not see how their marriage could survive. She consulted a lawyer for advice as she prepared herself for the divorce she believed inevitable.

The following Sunday Delia was at church, again without Jamie, when the preacher highlighted the biblical teaching on marriage and divorce. To begin with, Delia found his insights helpful and illuminating, but she began to feel increasingly uncomfortable as she heard him stress the permanence of marriage (Gen 2:24). These are words which Jesus endorsed, adding that divorce was allowable in God's eyes only when one partner is sexually unfaithful. Delia knew that this was not the problem she faced, so made an appointment to see her minister to discuss the situation.

Their conclusion, as they reflected on her circumstances, was that neither the spiritual incompatibility, nor the deterioration in their relationship, were grounds enough to consider divorce. God had recognised their union at the time of their marriage, and Delia's minister took time to encourage her to catch a fresh vision of what God could make of her marriage, and to pray constantly that Jamie would become a Christian. He said, however, that the final decision as to whether or not she sought the divorce had to be hers...

A Prayer Please help me, Lord, to be able to see my situation at home clearly, and with insight that comes from you. Save me, I pray, from making any decisions, one way or the other, that later I shall regret.

A Practical Suggestion Find something positive and constructive you can do today to help improve your situation at home – even if it is small.

Setting an Example

We did this…to make ourselves a model for you to follow
(2 Thessalonians 3:9)

Read: 2 Thessalonians 3:6-10

Cathy was becoming increasingly disillusioned because Robbie seemed completely disinterested in the Christian faith that was so important to her. In fact, she was becoming so frustrated that one day, in her women's prayer group, she expressed herself quite angrily and at some length. 'If my Christian life is so pathetic that Robbie can't see how I've changed since I've become a Christian, is it worth carrying on?' After the meeting the pastor's wife took Cathy on one side. 'Please don't do that again', she said. 'If you feel uptight, come and talk to me privately. Do you realise the effect what you said would have had on Lindsay?'

To be honest, Cathy had not given Lindsay a moment's thought. Lindsay had only been a Christian for a few weeks, but was absolutely sure that God's first task for her was to witness to her unbelieving husband. Cathy realised as she thought about it afterwards that she could have seriously discouraged Lindsay by what she had said. 'Please remember', the pastor's wife continued, 'that as the older Christian, you have a responsibility to be a role model for those who have come to faith more recently.'

Cathy had never considered this before, but it made sense to her. Paul taught the same vital truth. He knew how helpful it is when Christians who struggle to follow Jesus and become more like him have human examples to emulate. We all need role models to follow, as well as being role models for others. That places an great responsibility on *us* as well as Cathy.

A Prayer Please help me to follow Jesus faithfully, Lord, but then to realise that he wants to use even me as a role model for others. Help me, please, to be an encouragement to others.

A Practical Suggestion List ways in which another Christian you know has modelled Jesus Christ to you since you became a believer.

Believing Prayer

If two of you on earth agree about anything you ask for, it will be done
(Matthew 18:19)

Read: Matthew 18:15-20

One day Hayley felt that God was leading her to pray harder for her family. She thought of her husband, George, whom she loved dearly, but who had not yet come to Christ, together with her two children, Alice and Paul, who were growing up fast. She wanted so much for her family unit to be solidly Christian, and found it hard to cope with things as they were.

On holiday, as the children threw stones into the still water of a lake, she noticed how, after the initial splash, circle after circle of ripples spread out over the surface of the water. Hayley thought of the impact that prayer makes when God answers the heartfelt requests of his children, and especially of the way that God works when Christians pool their prayers and pray together. That day, as never before, she realised how both the Bible and so many Christian books are full of stories of the faithful way that God responds to his children's sincere prayers.

Jesus taught that prayer is powerful and effective, especially when two or more of his disciples join forces to pray. Paul reassures us in 1 Timothy 2:4 that God wants everyone to come to know him. Therefore, when we pray for our friends and families to find Jesus Christ as their Saviour, we are praying in line with God's will. Who knows what will happen next as Hayley commits herself to pray more intensively than ever before?

A Prayer Please show me, Lord, how you want me to pray and who with. I ask you to respond to my plea that my whole family will come to love and trust you too.

A Practical Suggestion Find a group of three or four others who will join you in praying regularly for their families and yours (spouse, children, parents) to come to faith in Jesus Christ.

Going on Ahead

I am going...to prepare a place for you (John 14:2)

Read: John 14:1-6

A pained expression was visible on Gemma's face one morning as she knocked on her friend, Maureen's, door. With her husband at work, the children safely at school, and the washing-up done, Gemma had settled down in her favourite armchair with a cup of coffee and her Bible. However, instead of gaining reassurance, her Bible reading caused her some concern. In one sense this was surprising because Jesus was speaking of the preparations he is making for all his family to join him in heaven. This part of Jesus' teaching is virtually guaranteed to excite Christians...but not Gemma.

By no means was she feeling ungrateful to Jesus for what he had done and would do for her, but Gemma's pain concerned Geoff, her husband. He expressed mild interest in her faith, but only sufficient to ask the occasional question and to go to church with her occasionally. She loved him dearly, and desperately wanted him to believe in Jesus too, but so far he had made no decision to do so. 'What would happen if he had an accident and died suddenly?' she asked Maureen. 'Would he go to hell?'

Maureen had considerable difficulty in giving Gemma the reassurance she needed that day. Gemma would only accept the blunt truth of the Bible, and Maureen had to confirm that only those who personally trust Jesus will join him in heaven. Once Maureen had prayed for her, Gemma was more aware again of her own salvation, but she left her friend's home more committed than ever to praying for Geoff.

A Prayer I am grateful for the promise to me of life in heaven with you, Lord, I pray again for my husband. Please reveal yourself to him so that we can look forward to heaven together.

A Practical Suggestion Take some time to meditate on Jesus' words of reassurance about heaven. Think about what it will be like, and then pray that your husband asks you a question one day soon which will allow you to explain this to him.

The Big Test

Anyone who looks at a woman lustfully has already committed adultery with her in his heart (Matthew 5:28)

Read: 2 Samuel 11:1-27

Jenny could hardly contain her excitement. 'Oh', she gasped to Jeanette, who was sitting next to her in church. 'Gareth's preaching today, I'm so pleased'. Gareth was the youth leader in Jenny's church and preached only rarely. She found him extremely handsome with his boyish face, blond hair and suntan. He also had an impish sense of humour, was a lively and effective communicator and was obviously very close to God. In many ways he was everything that appealed to Jenny and was the virtual opposite to Frank, her husband, who resolutely refused to come to church, and sat at home glued to the sports channel on TV when he was not at work.

Things had gone further in Jenny's mind, however, than merely appreciating Gareth as a preacher. She allowed her mind to wander sometimes and wondered how he performed in bed. She considered it harmless to speculate. After all, life with Frank was boring, tedious and sometimes acrimonious. Why was it so wrong to get a little mental pleasure? The fact that Gareth was married was irrelevant; his pretty young wife was not affected by this. She gazed lustfully at Gareth as he began to preach, hardly hearing a word he said.

David's fling with Bathsheba was one of his biggest mistakes (v27). His adultery would never have taken place had he controlled his thoughts earlier on. The Lord forgave him when he repented (see Psalm 51), but God was sad at this serious indiscretion. Jenny needs to be very careful.

A Prayer Please help me, Lord, to control my thoughts and not to be deceived by Satan into thinking that adulterous thoughts are acceptable. Rather, show me how to pray positively for my husband.

A Question to Answer When you find yourself thinking or acting in a particular way, do you ask, 'Would Jesus behave like this?'

The Difference That Counts

What does a believer have in common with an unbeliever?
(2 Corinthians 6:15)

Read: 2 Corinthians 6:14-18

Megan had been far from happy when the minister of her church refused to marry her to Jonathan because, although she was a committed Christian, Jonathan was not. She felt it was unfair, but her minister saw their prospective marriage as contrary to the teaching of Scripture. He felt it was unwise for them to proceed, and impossible for the church to endorse the wedding and subsequent marriage. Eventually they decided to get married at a secular venue, but felt let down. Megan, meanwhile, was determined to prove that she could still grow spiritually and be on fire for God, although married to an unbeliever.

For the first few years she seemed to be doing well, but in the lead-up to their tenth wedding anniversary the strain was beginning to tell. Jonathan had had phases when he seemed more responsive to Christianity, but they did not last. As she read the Bible, in between her less frequent visits to church, Megan realised increasingly the truth of Paul's words which describe the incompatibility of believers and unbelievers. It was true. She and Jonathan had different priorities and goals, not only different moral standards, social interests and hobbies. It dawned on her that while she and Jonathan were moderately happy on the surface, they shared little at a deeper level.

This insight helped her to come to two conclusions. First, she realised that her church was not as unwise as she had thought originally. Secondly, she knew that she needed to pray all the more for Jonathan to get to know Jesus personally.

A Prayer Help me to face the reality of any past mistakes I have made, Lord, I pray. Forgive me as I confess, and strengthen me to keep growing in you.

A Practical Suggestion While you and your husband may have differences which concern you, look for something you can enjoy together in the next day or two.

Feeling Let Down

You would not listen to me (Jeremiah 38:15)

Read: Jeremiah 38:1-13

Fiona was doing her very best to convince her husband, Gerry, how important her faith was. She told him about Jesus' life, death and resurrection, and the difference that his forgiveness, peace, security and guidance made in her life each day. Even as she was speaking, she knew that Gerry was not really listening. His mind was clearly on other things, probably on the work that would occupy him the next morning. Fiona felt that she had wasted her breath. Gerry had been polite, but seemed to ignore completely the best news he would ever hear. If only he would really listen...

Jeremiah, God's prophet, had to contend with exactly the same frustration. All he ever sought to do was to relay faithfully God's word to God's people, yet they were persistently unresponsive. What Jeremiah could not grasp was why they could see their plight, but not recognise that trusting God was their only hope. His frustration reached an all-time high when he was imprisoned and later lowered into a well to die. His only crime had been to speak out God's word and truth.

Fiona, and others like her, have to recognise that those who need to hear God's word most may be among those who seem least inclined to receive it. However, God asks his people to faithfully declare it anyway. The ultimate responsibility for acting on it has to lie with the hearers. How sad for both Jeremiah and Fiona that their faithful words were not heeded...

A Prayer Please help me to be patient, Lord, when my words for you do not seem to elicit a response, but help me most of all to be faithful.

A Question to Answer If your husband really will not listen when you tell him about Jesus, are you sure it is not because you preach at him, tell him in the wrong way, too often or at the wrong time?

Effective Communication

Each one heard them speaking in his or her own language (Acts 2:6)

Read: Acts 2:1-16

Gill wanted God's special help. She was desperately keen for her husband to become a Christian, but she found that sometimes when she talked with him about anything spiritual, it was completely the wrong time. He was never deliberately awkward, but sometimes had work problems on his mind or he was tired. Occasionally, though, he entered into lengthy discussions with Gill about the reasons why he found coping with faith difficult. Her prayer was that God would give her a special gift of knowing when it was the best time to talk with Bryan. She always felt let down when a discussion ended before it had hardly begun.

On the Day of Pentecost the disciples of Jesus were given just such a gift. True, God's Spirit gave them the capacity to speak a variety of languages they had never learned, but the effect was that people who had not heard the good news of Jesus discovered all about him as the Holy Spirit equipped the disciples to communicate simply but powerfully. It was as the Holy Spirit worked behind the scenes that day that three thousand people committed their lives to Jesus.

Gill believed that as God had done it once he could do it again. Why should he not guide her as to when to speak and when to keep quiet? Why should the Holy Spirit, who knows what Bryan is thinking, not guide Gill as to what subject to raise for discussion? For the sake of Bryan's conversion and God's glory, Gill asked God for a special gift, and trusted him to respond positively.

A Prayer Give me, I pray, a similar gift of your Holy Spirit, Lord, so that I too may have that instinctive sense of what to say about you, when to speak and when to be quiet. Please bring my husband to faith in Jesus soon.

A Question to Answer Are you ready to be God's specific and sensitive mouthpiece at home? Tell God if you are.

Jesus' Response to Simple Faith

Don't be afraid; just believe (Mark 5:36)

Read: Mark 5:21-24; 35-43

Heather had a puzzled look on her face as she listened to her minister preach. He was explaining the extraordinary spiritual truth that although anything God does is due ultimately to his remarkable and awe-inspiring power, he often involves people by working in partnership with them. Of course God can work independently, but so often he chooses to share what he does with people, in response to their simple trust and faith. It dawned on Heather that God may be offering her such an opportunity in order to see John, her husband, become a Christian. Until now, he had staunchly declined to bite on the carefully-chosen and occasional words of witness she had expressed to him. Now, listening to the sermon, Heather's faith began to grow. If she simply trusted God for John to become a Christian and sought, with his help, to live as a Christian at home, then maybe in due course John would respond to Jesus.

The four Gospels show clearly how much emphasis Jesus placed on the faith of individuals being the trigger that allowed God's divine power to be released. Jairus had no doubt that Jesus could heal his daughter, and Jesus responded to this. Jesus' words, however, show that he was looking for faith in Jairus and his wife before the miracle would happen.

God still looks for simple trust in wives like Heather, whom he calls to work as his partners, so that, in his way and according to his timescale, he can do more miracles in people's lives.

A Prayer I recognise that faith is a spiritual gift, Lord. Please give me more.

A Question to Answer Can you believe that Jesus could draw your husband into a personal relationship with himself? If you struggle to answer, ask God for more faith.

The Pain of Separation

If the unbeliever leaves, let it be so (1 Corinthians 7:15)

Read: 1 Corinthians 7:1-16

Rosemary's eyes were red as she picked up the phone and called her minister, Frank. During a row the night before, her husband, Jeffrey, had walked out of the house saying that if she carried on believing this rubbish about a first-century Jew called Jesus, she would have to live alone. With that he left, and now, the next morning, she had no idea where he was. Rosemary had spent half the night sobbing into her pillow before falling asleep exhausted. Now she needed her minister's support.

Frank was keen to establish how much Rosemary's faith was really to blame in their relationship. Had she preached at Jeffrey insensitively? No. Had she always insisted on going to church every Sunday irrespective of his wishes? No. Had she demanded that he go to church with her or believe what she did? No. As Frank listened, he heard a sad story which showed that an essentially happy marriage had changed from the day Rosemary had first heard the gospel of Jesus. She had never expected to love Jesus in place of Jeffrey; she saw from the beginning how different the two relationships were. Her long-term prayer was that Jeffrey would want to love Jesus too so that they could be truly united spiritually.

Frank had to point Rosemary to 1 Corinthians 7, though they prayed together that Jeffrey would take time to reflect carefully on his marriage and what he stood to lose. What is more, Rosemary dared to pray that Jeffrey would work through his resistance to Christianity and come to Christ, whether he returned to her or not. That is a brave prayer to pray!

A Prayer Please minister very powerfully to me or any Christian wife who is in this sad situation, Lord. Help me to respond in a way that will help my husband to see your love in me.

A Question to Answer If you and your husband disagree about your faith, are you sure that is really the problem in your relationship – or is it just a symptom?

Rich Support

Guard my life, for I am devoted to you (Psalm 86:2)

Read: Psalm 86:1-13

Enid's patience was running thin because nothing seemed to be improving. She was fed up with the verbal abuse she had to tolerate at home from her husband. He had been in a state of rebellion and anger ever since she had first gone to an event at her local church, and that was three years before her conversion. For a reason she still did not fully understand, Stan had an aversion to religion, and Enid bore the brunt of his cynicism and temper. From the beginning she had struggled over how to cope with this, but because she did not want to let Stan down in front of her church friends, she kept quiet and suffered in silence.

Even so, she was not inactive. When she had free time at home she found that she could pour out her hurt, anger and frustration to God in the same way as the writer of Psalm 86 did centuries before. Both of them discovered the true sense of release there is in off-loading to God the problems they faced. The fact that she could be totally honest with God, without being disloyal, was liberating, but Enid wanted a solution. While God's presence and strength were resources she could not do without, she desperately wanted the situation at home to change.

In this she was like the Psalmist who wanted an 'answer' (v1) and salvation from his dilemma (v2). He had no doubt that God could and would heed his passionate prayer (v8,10), and Enid also found that her faith in God grew as she kept praying for a remedy.

A Prayer Work in my life by your Spirit, I pray, Lord, so that as I trust you, you can answer my deepest needs and glorify yourself.

A Practical Suggestion The writer of Psalm 86 was prepared to reaffirm his strong and loyal commitment to God *despite* his personal pain. Try this even if you do not feel like it. God will honour your commitment.

A Persuasive Argument

Do you think...you can persuade me to be a Christian? (Acts 26:28)

Read: Acts 26:1-32

Veronica was particularly interested in one session of a course she was doing that her church had organised. It was about the value of a personal testimony. At the end of the lesson, the leader suggested that everyone prepared their own story of how Jesus had worked in their life, and should come back next week ready to share it. Veronica found this an exciting challenge because since first hearing about Jesus, she had been forgiven her sins and healed of a painful physical complaint. Also, with God's help, she had given up both smoking and drinking to which she had been addicted. Writing down her testimony would be a great reminder of what God had done for her, especially as she would have a more complete story to share with Sam, her husband, who had only heard parts of it until now.

While the Apostle Paul's times in prison may have seemed an enormous hindrance and disadvantage at the time, they provided this pioneer missionary with many extra opportunities to tell the story of how Jesus had changed him. Indeed, so powerful was his testimony that King Agrippa found it very persuasive – and he was only listening to it in the context of a trial!

Many people have become Christians through hearing or reading about the way God has changed someone else. Who knows how Sam will respond when Veronica finds the right time to share her story? Having heard the gospel already, it may be just what he needs to remind him how much Veronica really has changed.

A Prayer Please show me how I can weave what you have done for me, Lord, into a compelling story that I can share with others, and especially my husband.

A Practical Suggestion As a useful exercise, write out your testimony, commit the main headlines to memory, then ask one of your Christian friends if you can 'practice' on them.

Putting Your Foot in it

How long will you keep getting drunk? (1 Samuel 1:14)

Read: James 3:1-12

There were many events in her life that Tanya wished had never happened or that, at least, she could now completely forget. In practice, though, the memories remained and sent cold shivers down her spine whenever she recalled them. One of the worst times was when she inadvertently asked the postman an ambiguous question, and another was when she got angry one Sunday and ended up shouting at the pastor on the church steps.

Eli was probably none too pleased with himself after he approached a praying woman at the temple and reprimanded her for being drunk. On this occasion no harm seems to have been done, but on others, people get hurt, angry, resentful and indignant when someone speaks out of turn.

If your deepest desire is to see your husband come to Christ, you will not want to ruin your witness at home by saying a lot of inappropriate things which you later regret. Imperfect people, even if they are redeemed sinners, still have plenty of capacity to foul things up. Tanya knew this, so when she learned that God could help her to tame her tongue, she asked him to do so, in order that her witness in front of Derek, her husband, was not compromised so often. Instinctively she knew that if she could conquer this problem to some extent he would possibly become a Christian sooner.

A Prayer Lord, I know that when my emotions are aroused I can say the most unfortunate things. With your help, I pray that I will be much more in control of myself so that I let you down by what I say much less often.

A Practical Suggestion Why not promise yourself and God that you will count to ten before you open your mouth and speak on occasions when you could become angry or when someone takes you by surprise?

A Passionate Plea

With many...words he pleaded with them' (Acts 2:40)

Read: Acts 2:14-16; 36-41

Diane had been a Christian for fourteen years and was on holiday with her family. They visited a wild life park one day and along with the animals, birds, pets corner, adventure playground and souvenir shop, they heard the owner speak about the need for increased conservation of some species of birds and mammals. What struck Diane most was the commitment which he had to protecting endangered species and the passion with which he spoke of the need for action on their behalf now.

However, his dedication was not merely verbal. He had given up a well-paid job, sold his family's home and taken out a bank loan in order to buy the land on which the wild life park now stood. What was more, he was also involved politically in trying to stop certain practices which were destroying the habitat of many endangered species world-wide. Yet, despite his words, it was his passionate pleas to his audience to help in this work of conservation that affected Diane most. She wondered how many more people, including her own husband, Joe, would be Christians by now if she and other Christians were deeply passionate for Christ and his work of mission.

On the Day of Pentecost it was not only the words Peter spoke in his historic sermon that led to three thousand people being converted to faith in Jesus Christ; his pleading with them made a difference too. Today we need more Christians with more passion to see others of their family and friends brought to Christ.

A Prayer Lord, please give me a real burden to see my family and friends come to you so that I do more to help bring them to you.

A Practical Suggestion If you would feel unnatural pleading with someone to become a Christian, think what it would be like telling someone else.

When to Submit

Wives should submit to their husbands in everything (Ephesians 5:24)

Read: Ephesians 5:21-6:4

In many parts of the world today, discussion that leads to mutual agreement is much more common than domination and obedience. Indeed, it may only be in animal training classes that the term 'obedience' is commonplace. It certainly surprised Geraldine when, having become a Christian, she heard these verses from Ephesians 5 being read in church. When she married Tom she did not promise in the vows to obey him. She thought that this concept of obeying your husband was something from the dark ages.

However, Christians believe that the Bible is God's revealed truth and should therefore form the basis of all that they are taught. What is more, many Christians realise that they should not attempt to simply fill their minds with this truth, but that it should govern their lifestyle too. This is what worried Geraldine. She was not sure how, as a new Christian, she should submit herself to Tom, her husband, who did not yet believe.

As she discussed her concern with her friends at church, Geraldine understood better that God demands her greatest love and loyalty. She also realised that he encourages her strongly to fully commit herself to her marriage, unless and until her husband makes demands of her that contradict her faith. True, she may have to cope with personal sacrifice sometimes, such as missing church because of his wishes. However, her goal is to love, honour and respect Tom, so that he sees Jesus Christ in her and responds himself to God's call.

A Prayer Desiring more than anything, Lord, that my husband finds you, I pray for your grace and love, so that I live such a compelling life as a Christian that he will want to love and trust you too. Please help him to notice Jesus in me!

A Question to Answer Is there any irritating habit or tendency you have, about which your husband comments, but which you would be willing to try to change to help show him that you love him?

Getting it Right

I know that the Lord has given this land to you (Joshua 2:9)

Read: Joshua 2:1-14

Jane's constant problem was where her loyalty should ultimately lay. Her specific and long-term goal was that Dave, whom she had married seven years before, should become a Christian, as she had done three years earlier. In the short-term, when Dave wanted to go out for the day on Sundays, she agreed, but only reluctantly. She would much rather have been at church, and always felt guilty for being absent. She felt torn, but deep down, however, she was totally committed to her marriage and God. What she kept thrashing around in her mind was, 'Where should my ultimate loyalty lie?'

Rahab (possibly an innkeeper and not necessarily a prostitute) was a source of inspiration to Jane. She lived in a city which God intended to be taken by his Israelite people. Hebrews tells us that her faith in God was so strong that even though she was a resident of Jericho, she believed the prediction of the Israelite spies and co-operated fully with them. Rahab's reward was not only to be saved when the city was destroyed, but also, after her death, to be included in the catalogue of people who have demonstrated great faith in God (Heb 11:31).

Rahab discerned that the eternal dimension is ultimately the most important. Jane, and other wives in her situation, have to make their own decisions as to what to do when there is a conflict between their short-term and long-term priorities, but the same God is there to guide them as guided Rahab.

A Prayer When I find it hard to make decisions, Lord, help me to sense what is the right thing to do in order to help the present situation, and, more importantly, what course to take that will help your long-term plans for my husband and me to flourish.

A Question to Answer Have you ever specifically asked God to show you what his long-term plans are for your life? If not, ask him now.

God's Strength in our Weakness

When I am weak, then I am strong (2 Corinthians 12:10)

Read: 2 Corinthians 12:1-10

Avril felt particularly despondent as she sat in her armchair by the fire. When she married Brian over twenty years earlier they were both committed and enthusiastic Christians. However, it was now well over a decade that she had been going to church alone. Brian no longer had any personal faith in God, and, due partly to his feelings of guilt, their relationship became strained whenever they attempted to discuss anything to do with Christianity or church. What Avril needed more than anything was God's reassurance. As well as sadness, she felt drained.

God's Apostle, Paul, felt low at times too. On one occasion he pleaded with God to remove a problem from his life, but instead of answering the prayer as Paul expected, God told him that whenever he was feeling weak, inadequate or vulnerable, he was potentially in a position of enormous strength. Paul learned from experience that Christians at their weakest and lowest are prime candidates to receive huge injections of God's energy and power.

Sadly, there are many Christians who feel sad because of a painful situation at home. Like Avril, they sense they are getting nowhere, and they cannot see any light at the end of the tunnel. God wants to encourage Avril and others like her, as he did Paul. If they abandon whatever resources they feel they have left and they open themselves to God, he can transform their future as his power, hope and vision fill them. Then they will be able to cope – whatever happens.

A Prayer When I feel despondent, Lord, I often lose faith in what you can do. Forgive me, I pray, and help me to turn over my weakness to you so that you can fill me again with your dynamic power.

A Practical Suggestion List all the things that God may see as a hindrance to him working in your life. Pray through each one, asking God to take away all that is unhelpful, and then invite him to give you a fresh injection of his power.

Praying for Results

Other seed fell on good soil. It came up, grew and produced a crop (Mark 4:8)

Read: Mark 4:1-20

Gillian found her mind wandering as her church's house group was going on around her. During a series of studies on Jesus' parables, the group was looking now at Jesus' story of the sower, and considering the different kinds of soil on which the seed fell. As each one was discussed, Gillian tried to identify which was the nearest to Alex, her husband, who, while still an unbeliever, attended church more often now. This meant that he was having the seed of the gospel sown into his mind quite frequently, and what was preoccupying Gillian as the small group study continued was how she could help change whichever kind of ground Alex was now into the 'good soil' which produced 'a crop'.

Did Alex represent the path where Satan 'takes away the word that was sown' (v4/15)? Was he more like the 'rocky places' where the word is received with joy, but then abandoned when difficulties arise (v5-6; 16-17)? Maybe Alex was like the thorns where worldly concerns and other priorities swamp any emerging life in the new plant (v7; 18-19). Gillian struggled to categorise Alex, but promised herself and God that she would pray for discernment in the next few days.

The conclusion reached by Gillian about Alex is between her and God. The benefit of Gillian praying this through is that she can now pray more specifically for him, and pray against whatever distractions are hindering his becoming 'good soil' – which is the point at which he will make a genuine, deep and informed commitment of his life to Jesus.

A Prayer Please give me, Lord, that ability to see and understand what is hindering my husband from coming to faith in Jesus. Then show me what to pray for and against.

A Question to Answer Is God calling you to do anything that would make it easier for your husband to commit his life to Jesus?

A Risky Choice

Jonah ran away from the Lord (Jonah 1:3)

Read: Jonah 1:1-17

Stephanie had had about as much as she could take and was sorely tempted to abandon what she was constantly encouraged to do by her friends at church. They wanted her to keep witnessing to her husband, but she knew that Bobby was a very long way from ever believing in anything. He was a hard-working man whose pride prevented him from trusting anyone but himself and his ability to cope and provide. Now, however, following yet another row, Stephanie felt that it was all pointless. It would be much easier, and lead to more peace at home, if she just kept her faith to herself, gave up on church and certainly abandoned all attempts to see Bobby come to faith. The temptation to give up was enormous, and Stephanie felt the decision was almost made.

Centuries before, Jonah had been called by God to tell people about his faith. What is more, when it came to the crunch, he did not feel he could rise to the challenge God placed before him – which is why he left in the opposite direction. We only have to see the extraordinary lengths God went to in using a big fish, to see that he does not take kindly to missionaries who contemplate abandoning their calling.

What Stephanie needs is support, prayer and plenty of encouragement if she is not to become a modern-day Jonah. That puts a big responsibility on her Christian friends as well as her.

A Prayer You have put me in my home with a special missionary task to fulfil, Lord. Please strengthen me and remind me of my calling whenever I am tempted to give up and take an easier path.

A Question to Answer Before you give up on God's calling to you at home, have you stopped to consider everything he has ever done for you? Try making a list. You will find it a tremendous source of encouragement. Why not keep it as a bookmark in your Bible?

The Pain of Trial

Take your son, your only son...sacrifice him (Genesis 22:2)

Read: Genesis 22:1-14

While Lucy was really glad to be a Christian and her life now had much more meaning than before, she struggled every time she became aware of the pain she had deep inside because her husband did not share her faith. Lucy had a long-standing tendency to be pessimistic. When she became a follower of Jesus she found herself thinking of all the negative implications affecting Ian. Lucy and Ian had married seventeen years earlier, and she knew that because God had not forgiven Ian, he was destined to spend eternity separated from God and her. This thought was intolerable and sometimes occupied her mind continually and made her miserable. Friends called it 'a trial'; Lucy just wished it would go away.

Abraham's trial was painful. He was called by God to sacrifice the son he knew had been a special gift from God. Abraham was certain that through Isaac God's promise that he would become the father of 'a great nation' (Gen 12:2) would be fulfilled. Therefore, he could see no logic in God's instructions to sacrifice his son but, because he trusted God, he made plans to do so. He believed God would not fail him, and he did not.

Lucy needed to see her situation differently. While what she was going through was undoubtedly 'a trial', she would have done better to see it as an opportunity to pray positively for God to work in Ian's life, rather than focusing on her pain. This could turn around her whole attitude, and make her far more available to work with God to help Ian into his family and kingdom.

A Prayer Help me, Lord, I pray, not to resent the hard parts of my Christian life, but to look for positive opportunities to see you work in and through them.

A Question to Answer As you look at your life at the moment, are there any different, creative ways in which you could serve God? Are there talents you could develop in his service?

The Best Last

You have saved the best till now (John 2:10)

Read: John 2:1-11

Carol's greatest concern was how much longer her present nightmare would last. While there were times at home when life could be quite normal, there were others when, for no obvious reason, trouble flared. What made it worse was that, according to her husband, Sam, Carol's friends from church were to blame for everything. Carol knew that their children, Joanne and Martin, eight and six respectively, could do without the trauma, and her most frequent prayer to God was that their marriage would hold together, at least while the children were young. Carol knew that the family's problem was essentially nothing to do with her church friends, and she was praying for Jesus somehow to intervene.

He does sometimes. At the wedding in Cana, Jesus took an intriguing course of action, preventing a catastrophe at what was meant to be a celebration. Had he not done so, the family whose wedding it was would have inherited a negative reputation in the community for running out of wine. Jesus' miracle saved the day and completely transformed the situation.

In Cana, Jesus acted in an unpredictable way; no one would have guessed what he would do. It was often like this during his three years of public ministry. People could never tell whose life would be the next to be revolutionised. It could be Carol's, because, with his grace and power, Jesus loves to surprise people who trust him. His call to Carol, and others like her, is to keep trusting, keep praying – and wait.

A Prayer While I would be so thrilled if my husband became a Christian today, Lord, I recognise that this miracle will not happen according to my timetable, but yours. Strengthen me so that I can remain faithful to you however long it takes.

A Practical Suggestion When you next go to church, as you sing, pray and listen to God's Word, count up the number of rich expressions of love that God is giving to you.

God's Promised Presence

The angel went to her and said... 'The Lord is with you' (Luke 1:28)

Read: Luke 1:26-38

Eve was desperate. After twenty-six years of marriage, all but one of them as a Christian, Eve was slowly coming to the conclusion that Henry would never share her faith. He seemed as resistant now as ever. Indeed, his cynicism about all religions had never abated, despite seeing Eve gradually transformed from the nervous, hesitant girl he married into the gentle but confident wife and mother she was now. He seemed to think that there was no link between her growing faith and her growing self-confidence. She knew otherwise.

Eve prayed every day for Henry, sometimes more out of a sense of duty than in the belief that the man she loved would be changed by the risen Christ. Then one day, as she prayed, something unique happened. She felt a warm glow and sensed in a new way the reassuring and peaceful presence of Jesus. Joy surged up within her and she praised God, realising that he was meeting her where she was, and letting her know that he was listening to her prayers. She was not alone with her pain.

The Bible tells of numerous occasions when desperate people called to God and he responded in a tangible way. With a unique calling ahead of her, Mary received the message of reassurance brought to her by God's angel. Throughout history, people have testified how, usually totally unexpectedly, God has broken into their lives to give fresh hope and the promise of his future presence. Who knows where he may work next?

A Prayer I am very open to you, Lord, if you want to break into my life to say or share anything. Help me to be receptive to anything you want to say to me, in whatever way you choose.

A Practical Suggestion Make sure you do not spend all of your prayer time talking to God. Take time to be quiet and still. Then listen carefully. Write down anything you think God may be saying to you, and reflect on it.

God's Rich Love

How beautiful you are, my darling! Oh, how beautiful (Song of Songs 1:15)

Read: Songs of Songs 1:1-17

Jane felt guilty. She was not sure why, but thought it was related to the fact that many of the friends she met at the school gate were unhappy in their marriages. However, Jane was very content with Sean. They were attracted to each other initially because they shared similar interests and their personalities were similar enough to ensure that they rarely disagreed vehemently about anything. They had a healthy respect for each other, made time to talk, and planned regular date-nights. After seven years of marriage they were at least as passionately in love as they were when they were courting.

The only major issue that divided Jane and Sean was her faith. She became a Christian four years after they married, but while Sean had examined Christianity, he was reluctant to commit himself. They didn't ever argue about Jane's faith; it was more that she was prepared to commit herself to Christ then, whereas Sean felt he needed more time. However, at the school gate Jane felt guilt that she and Sean were genuinely happy, and sometimes wondered how God felt about their love for one another.

A friend then suggested that she read Song of Songs, and at first she found it hard to believe that so much romantic love was expressed in the Bible. However, she felt God reassure her that love was his gift to people to share and enjoy, but she also felt God call her to pray that Sean would soon come to see it like this, not merely as a human phenomenon.

A Prayer I pray that you will help me to appreciate the love I share with my husband, Lord. Show me how we can encourage it to grow and deepen more.

A Practical Suggestion Set some time aside so that you and your husband can make last-minute plans to do something spontaneous together that you will both enjoy.

They Just Do Not Understand

Were not all ten cleansed? Where are the other nine? (Luke 17:17)

Read: Luke 17:11-19

Pauline's Christian faith meant so much to her and she just could not understand her husband's assessment of it. To her, sin, repentance, forgiveness, trust in Jesus and spiritual guidance all made so much sense and seemed so obvious. Trevor merely saw Christianity as 'a fairy tale' and said that he had enough of religion as a child when he was brought up as a Catholic. He encouraged Pauline to go to church, but was totally unenthusiastic about doing so himself. Pauline had explained her faith to him many times and could not see why he could not and would not accept it for himself.

Jesus did not understand all the people of his day either. Ten men with leprosy had pleaded with him to heal them and he did so. As they went to show themselves to a priest who would confirm their freedom from the disease, they were miraculously cured. Excited as they all obviously were, only one of them, a foreigner, took the time and trouble to find Jesus again and thank him. This perplexed Jesus, who could not understand why the others had not come back.

The behaviour of other people will obviously confuse us too. We cannot see inside other people's minds and therefore Pauline, for example, may never grasp why Trevor cannot see what is so obvious to her. Like Jesus we may be bewildered, but we can continue to pray.

A Prayer Lord, when the behaviour of other people baffles me, help me to keep my eyes primarily on you because I know that you act consistently for our good.

A Practical Suggestion To ensure that you do not take Jesus and his love to you for granted, why not list the things he has done for you and your family, and for which you are grateful...now!

A Divine Summons

When the Lord saw that he had gone over to look, God called to him
(Exodus 3:4)

Read: Exodus 3:1-10

Alexandra found it difficult to know how forthright she should be with her husband and his family who as yet did not believe in Jesus as she did. She knew, of course, that Jesus' mandate for all his disciples was to go and make disciples (Matt 28:19), but when it came to how and when she should do this with Kevin, she was uncertain. She wondered if she should come home from church every Sunday and tell him what it had been about, or whether she should tell him about her daily Bible study and prayer-time on the days when it was especially inspiring. She asked God for his help; she wanted him to guide her.

God had a special and unique task for Moses to do too. He was to represent God before Pharaoh, king of Egypt, and speak what God wanted him to say. The problem was that God did not yet have Moses' attention, which meant that Moses was not yet attuned to his voice. God needed to attract his attention before he could communicate anything and, uniquely on this occasion, opted to use a flaming bush that did not burn.

God's way of guiding Alexandra will be different. He speaks to people today in a variety of ways. This includes counsel from other Christians, as well as directly from the Holy Spirit as we read the Bible and pray. What is certain is that by one means or another God will guide Alexandra just as surely as, many generations before, he led Moses.

A Prayer When I am not sure what kind of approach or strategy is best in my situation at home, Lord, please show me your way.

A Question to Answer How many different ways can you think of that you and your friends have experienced God speaking to you since you became Christians? Try to find out.

Living In An Unfair World

Stephen, full of the Holy Spirit, looked up to Heaven and saw the glory of God (Acts 7:55)

Read: Acts 6:8-15; 7:51-60

Lynn was unusually quiet during her house fellowship meeting. When the group of seven women first began to meet about five years earlier, only one of them had a Christian husband. Now, today, Lynn was feeling isolated. All her friends were excited because Hilary's husband, Josh, had committed his life to Jesus the previous weekend. Hilary was exuberant, and everyone was elated, except Lynn, who, while trying to smile, felt the odd one out. This group had committed itself to pray the six men into God's kingdom; now five had responded, and the women were excited that God was answering prayer.

Lynn found herself trying to handle a number of simultaneous reactions. First, she was concerned that now the group would concentrate mainly on providing mutual support for women whose husbands were new Christians. Secondly, she thought that she would feel isolated and different. When these thoughts came into her mind, she began to feel anger welling up inside. It was not fair; she did not deserve this. It was not her fault that Terry, her husband, was not remotely interested in her faith.

Stephen's martyrdom was grossly unfair too – far more so, of course, than Lynn's situation. What Stephen found was that God compensated him in a wonderfully rich way for his human disadvantage. He was given a glimpse into heaven itself – something very unusual, and hardly what Lynn could expect. However, in his own way and out of his love, God may well have special encouragements for Lynn. He certainly does not want her to feel isolated.

A Prayer Help me, Lord, I pray, if I find I am disadvantaged through no obvious fault of my own. Give me new strength to cope, I ask.

A Question to Answer Can you think of any of your friends who may feel disadvantaged for reasons which are not of their own making? If so, pray for them and see if there is anything practical you can do to help.

Not Giving Up

Keep on speaking (Acts 18:9)

Read: Acts 18:1-11

Debbie felt that God was urging her to witness occasionally, yet positively, about her faith to her husband, John, and she did. She was careful to pick her moments but, when the right occasion came, she told him what Jesus meant to her. She explained how he wanted to bless their marriage, how he answered her prayers, and what a lot of joy she got from being part of the church. She was careful always to work out in advance what she would tell John, and was sensitive, avoiding comments that might appear to him to be critical of him or their marriage. She wanted to encourage the man she loved, not deflate him or drive him further from Christ.

John's reaction to Debbie's testimony varied. Sometimes he listened; at other times he stopped her mid-way. It seemed that his mood determined how much he could cope with. Even when he stopped Debbie, he was not intentionally unkind, although sometimes she felt frustrated.

Paul must have felt frustrated too when the Jews at Corinth rejected his message. God's words to him in a vision one night must have given him renewed confidence that he was doing the right thing. Certainly God wants his servants to keep on telling others about his love and grace. Their task is to remain faithful, and they should talk sensitively about his love to those who do not know him personally. Debbie must not give up, but she needs to pick her moments as carefully as possible.

A Prayer Give me the confidence and boldness I need to speak out for you, Lord. Guide me as to when I should speak and when I should remain silent. Let my words bear fruit for your kingdom.

A Practical Suggestion When you feel that God is calling you to witness for him, if you have advanced warning, pray through and plan in your mind (and maybe on paper) the sort of things you want to say. Then when the time comes, quietly ask God to guide every word you speak.

Opening Blind Eyes

They received their sight and followed him (Matthew 20:34)

Read: Matthew 20:29-34

Annie knew precisely what she was praying for. Two years earlier, after her friend Sylvia had told her about Jesus for the umpteenth time, suddenly it had made sense to her. It was as if someone had turned the light on. She understood why Christians get excited about Jesus and now, along with a growth in her faith, she was praying increasingly for her husband, Roger's, conversion too. Her constant request to God was that the light would be switched on for Roger too. Her plea was that Jesus would provide divine illumination for him just as he had done for her. She knew that the moment this happened, Roger would start to trust in Jesus personally too.

When Jesus was engaged in ministry on earth, he healed many blind eyes. People who had lived their lives in blackness, or whose sight was severely impaired, suddenly found that the shapes separated and the colours became distinguishable. Life could now be lived as God intended instead of trying to negotiate the many hazards with which visually impaired people have to cope. Annie had the faith to believe Jesus can still heal physically blind eyes, so why should he not open spiritually blind eyes? Why should Jesus not do for Roger what he had already done for her?

It was this spiritual logic that prompted Annie to commit herself to praying more intently than ever before for Roger. One day, Roger may be more grateful for this than words can express.

A Prayer Please help me to be faithful to you, Lord, whatever you ask me to pray for. Keep stimulating and encouraging my faith, I pray, so that you can glorify your name.

A Practical Suggestion Consider making a covenant with God that you will pray daily for your husband to come to faith – until he does. Maybe you can put your commitment on paper and sign it to show that you are serious.

Free From Guilt

If we confess our sins, he...will forgive us our sins (1 John 1:9)

Read: 1 John 1:5-2:2

Jocelyn had been an active and committed Christian for over a decade before she realised that there was some unfinished business between her and God with which she had to deal. She had grown up in a Christian family, had become a Christian aged ten, but had had a spiritually lean period in her later teens. At twenty-one she had recommitted herself to the Lord, and two years later had met Gary whom soon she decided to marry. He was sympathetic to her faith and supported her, but never committed his life to Christ.

Jocelyn kept growing as a Christian and was determined to prove that she was at no disadvantage being married to someone who did not share her faith. At the time of their marriage, she had rationalised that passages like Deuteronomy 7:3-4 and 2 Corinthians 6:14-16 did not apply to her and that, anyway, 1 Corinthians 7:14 taught that her husband would somehow become 'sanctified' through her. It was only many years later that she understood more. Engaged in a Bible study with some Christian women friends, she saw that the Bible teaches against spiritually-mixed marriages. God knows that occasionally an unbeliever will come to faith through their marriage relationship, but that often the spiritual life of the believer will suffer.

Recognising her earlier pride, rebellion and disobedience, Jocelyn repented humbly and sincerely before God. It was her birthday, and the gift of forgiveness she received was better than any other present!

A Prayer Where I have been disobedient, Lord, please forgive me as I confess my sin. Then use me for your glory as never before, especially to help my husband to find you.

A Question to Answer Do you believe Jesus can forgive you for *anything* you have done, thought or said wrongly? He can – and wants to!

Gaining Fresh Hope

I will bring health and healing (Jeremiah 33:6)

Read: Jeremiah 33:1-16

If you looked at Gloria, you would almost certainly never know how hard she found life. In fact, behind her front door things were very difficult for her and her partner, Sam. They had cohabited for many years. Then Gloria became a Christian through a friend at work, and gradually as she grew in faith, she felt that it was not just her who wanted her unhappy life to improve; God did too. Gloria and Sam had always argued a lot, but had remained together, but increasingly Gloria sensed that this was not normal, and nor was it right for them to share a home and bed without being married. She was desperate to see things change, yet Sam was unresponsive when she tried to talk with him. However, despite her dilemma, Gloria had a deep assurance that God knew about her situation, loved her and ultimately would work things out for her and Sam. That made a lot of difference.

Jeremiah had an incredibly difficult situation to live with too. Jerusalem was under siege, the people were disillusioned, Jeremiah himself was in prison, and he knew things would get much worse before God's promises of healing, forgiveness and restoration came to pass. Despite this, he was able to cope with his present pain because he knew God was going to work powerfully in the future.

God still gives hope in situations where darkness seems to reign but, like Jeremiah, we can open ourselves to hear God's word of hope – and then believe it!

A Prayer Help me to catch a vision for your future, Lord. Show me a glimpse of what you can do – especially in my husband's life.

A Question to Answer Have you read any section of the Bible recently which describes God's great power and strength? If not, it could be a good use of some time today! Try reading one or two of the Psalms that spell out how majestic God is.

A Solid Foundation

The winds blew and beat against that house, yet it did not fall (Matthew 7:25)

Read: Matthew 7:24-29

The biggest concern Josie had was that her three youngsters, Sophie, Rachel and Adam, would not hear much about Jesus during their formative years. David, her husband, was not especially anti-Christian; rather, he felt that just because Josie was a Christian herself, there was no reason for her to brainwash the children. He felt that no one should be indoctrinated about what to believe, and that just as he and Josie had had the opportunity to make up their own minds about Christianity, so should their children.

However, instinctively, Josie was less than certain that such a policy was a responsible one. She opposed indoctrination too, but felt it was her duty as a Christian parent, albeit a new one, to teach her children who Jesus was, and what he offers today to people who trust him. She could not believe this would do them any harm; on the contrary, it would provide them with the firmest foundation of all on which to build their future lives.

Jesus was in no doubt that the only way to live a fulfilled and satisfying life, which is also secure and stable, is for us to base our lives on him and his teaching. If we do so, we will have God's strength within us and will be able to withstand the storms that afflict us. Even though she had only been a Christian for two years, Josie had experienced this – which was why she wanted her children to grow up enjoying the same opportunity.

A Prayer Please help me, Lord, to live the kind of life that Jesus describes here. Then help others, and especially my family, to see in me, I pray, how fulfilling and worthwhile it is to trust you.

A Question to Answer As you reflect on your life since you became a Christian, what differences can you see in yourself that indicate what God has done for you? Thank God for all the good things you have seen.

A Man's Man

Jesus...called to him those he wanted, and they came to him (Mark 3:13)

Read: Mark 3:13-19

Whatever she did Brenda could not persuade Joe to have anything to do with her church. Every time she tried to get him to join her, he reminded her that when he was taken as a child, the church was full of little children and old ladies with old-fashioned hats. Men were a rare sight – apart from the vicar, of course, and he spoke in a strange sing-along voice that seemed to Joe to be utterly false. If this was Christianity, then at the tender age of nine, he had decided that he wanted nothing to do with it.

Brenda knew she had an uphill struggle. Her goal was to help Joe to see how much of a man's man Jesus was. There was nothing effeminate about him, and in order to prepare for the continuance of his work once he had completed his role on earth and returned to heaven, he chose a group of men who were among the toughest and strong-willed around to share in his ministry. In no way did he exclude women from his life, but he opted to share with men the specific task of developing on earth the work he had begun.

To convince Joe to look again at Christianity, but this time in a different light, was never going to be quick for Brenda. She resolved, however, to show him, bit by bit, that the most masculine man of all, and one well worth following, was the one he was refusing to acknowledge.

A Prayer Help me to show to my husband and other people I know who do not yet believe in Jesus, what kind of person he really is so that they can make their own response based on accurate information.

A Practical Suggestion Without having to strain things, see if you can arrange for your husband to meet some men from your church in a relaxed social environment.

The Power of Prayer

As long as Moses held up his hands, the Israelites were winning
(Exodus 17:11)

Read: Exodus 17:8-16

Gail was wondering if it was all worthwhile. She had been challenged at church to pick a specific need she had and to pray about it at more length and with possibly greater intensity than usual. The church's Prayer Thrust had been introduced to stimulate more praying by the fellowship, and Gail had committed herself to pray for Phil, her husband, who showed only slight interest in anything spiritual. She really believed that within a week she would see a noticeable change.

However, two weeks later nothing had happened. Phil seemed totally unchanged. He was still as helpful as ever around the house but showed no more interest than before in Gail's faith. She expressed her disappointment to her friend, Kath, who reminded her that God has a timetable which we neither know nor understand. His plan of things is so different from ours. Moses raised his hands to commend symbolically to God the battle against the Amalekites in the valley below, and God honoured him. In the same way God continues to respond to heartfelt prayers brought to him by those who sincerely want him to be glorified on earth.

After this, Gail continued to pray for Phil just as passionately as before, but now she was prepared to wait for God to answer in his own time. Her role was to pray faithfully however long it took. Interestingly, she sensed that as she prayed daily for Phil that she was being drawn closer to both him and God.

A Prayer Please help me, Lord, to be one of your most faithful and determined prayer warriors as I regularly commit my family, and especially my husband, to you.

A Practical Suggestion If you struggle to pray as consistently as you would like, look at your whole day, decide when is the best time to devote to talking with God, pick a conducive place – and then go for it!

Trying to Stay Together

They will become one flesh (Genesis 2:24)

Read: Genesis 2:18-25

Geraldine was devastated, angry and disgusted when she arrived at her pastor's wife's front door. For a while, she had been slightly suspicious that something unusual was going on, but she never seriously thought that Robert, her husband of eight years, would betray her. She had confronted him after dinner, and had refused to accept his evasive answers. To her horror, she learned that for a few months he had been having an affair with a family friend. Having heard as much as she could cope with, Geraldine rushed for the door and soon, tear-stained and nearly hysterical, arrived to pour out her pain.

With sensitive help and care she began to grasp the seriousness of Robert's actions, and it was not long before she asked Kath, her pastor's wife, whether she ought to leave Robert for good and seek a divorce. Kath refused to advise her, but wanted Geraldine to understand that, biblically, Robert's actions seemed to be grounds for divorce. Yet it could be that Robert, who had often been to church but never made a profession of faith, might repent and ask Geraldine to give him another chance.

Kath reminded Geraldine how God sees marriage as permanent, although he allows for the possibility of divorce because, sadly, people are not always able to keep their promises. She showed Geraldine that if Robert were to repent and she still loved him and could forgive him, God would be glad. So far, despite Robert's serious indiscretion, God still saw them as one.

A Prayer Help me to forgive, Lord, if I have been hurt and sinned against. Please heal my painful wounds, and fill me with your extraordinary love.

A Question to Answer Have you ever thought how much God loves you and to what extent he has forgiven you? Sit and think about it.

The Remarkable Plans of God

Joseph, the husband of Mary, of whom was born Jesus (Matthew 1:16)

Read: Matthew 1:1-17

Jasmine was puzzled. She could not understand why, as she prayed about it, that her husband had not become a Christian too. After all, she had read that God 'wants all men to be saved and to come to a knowledge of the truth' (1 Tim 2:4), so she believed that it must be God's will. What puzzled her was that thirteen years after her conversion, Jim, her husband, had still not made a personal commitment of his own.

The beginning of Matthew's Gospel helps us to see things in perspective. For the benefit of his Jewish readers, Matthew details the way that God has ordered the life of his Jewish people so that a direct family line links Abraham, through David, to Jesus 'who is called Christ'. Matthew's purpose in cataloguing what some might perceive as the most boring part of the New Testament, is that we can see how, for century after century and in generation after generation, God has been working out the plans he conceived before time began.

It is by no means unusual for people like Jasmine to be concerned that they cannot see the progress being made here and now that they would choose. However, at the end of the day, while naturally wanting God to bring many more people into his kingdom, we can do no more than trust, pray and co-operate with God in any way he asks. Only he can fulfil his plans, and he does so in his own time-scale.

A Prayer Help me, Lord, to trust you even when I do not understand what does or does not seem to be happening. Please give me your perspective on my marriage.

A Question to Answer If God was able to organise it so that his Son, Jesus, was born in just the right place to the right people at the right time, and in fulfilment of hundreds of earlier prophesies, do you not think he can work in your husband's life?

Surprise, Surprise!

He invited Philip to come up and sit with him (Acts 8:31)

Read: Acts 8:26-40

You could have knocked Barbara down with a feather! She and Steve had been married four years, during which time she had begun to follow Jesus. This was never a problem to Steve, and he sometimes accompanied Barbara to special events held at the church she began to attend. However, as far as she was concerned, Steve's level of interest in religion in general, and Christianity in particular was small. What she did not know was that while she was at work some days and he was at home alone, he was reading the Christian books she brought into the house. Gradually, Steve was being drawn closer, and one day, as he knelt beside their bed, he committed his life to loving and serving Jesus. When, some weeks later, he plucked up courage to tell Barbara, she was more ecstatic than words can describe!

Like Barbara, Philip was astounded by the way God works. Philip would not have understood to begin with why he had to leave the spiritual revival in Samaria to go out into the desert. Yet it all started to make sense when the Ethiopian came by reading about the Suffering Servant, but not understanding anything about him. Philip wasted no time in telling him, led the man to Christ, and baptised him in an oasis in the desert. Philip always knew that this amazing conversion was a result of God's gentle work of preparation, and very little to do with him.

Who knows where God may work next?

A Prayer While I am tempted to try to take control of situations, help me to see Lord, that only when your Holy Spirit works in people's lives do they really begin to understand about you. Do something rich in my husband's life, I ask.

A Practical Suggestion However frustrated you may be because it seems that your husband's spiritual progress is slow or non-existent, try praying more – not manipulating more.

Becoming Hot Again

You are neither cold nor hot (Revelation 3:15)

Read: Revelation 3:14-22

Teresa did not like going to church at all, but because her children enjoyed their activities she felt obliged to take them. Once, about fifteen years earlier as a teenager, she had committed her life to Jesus Christ. However, since then she had devoted herself to her career, and more recently to her marriage and her role as a mother. She knew Jesus was an important teacher, but felt apathetic about him and his church.

One Sunday as she sat reluctantly in church, Teresa found herself compelled to really listen to the sermon. It was not that the preacher was especially eloquent; it was more that he had a conviction and passion which shone through in his message. His deep concern was that the church should penetrate the local community with the love of Jesus, but for that to happen, it would demand the whole-hearted commitment of those who were already part of God's family. He challenged each individual Christian to consider where they stood before God, and if necessary to repent and rededicate themselves to him.

Teresa began to reflect on how she had wasted what God had done earlier in her life. Her love for him was lukewarm, if that. Her husband, together with most of his family, and certainly their neighbours, had no concept of God's love for them at all. As God spoke to Teresa she began to cry, but she reaffirmed in church that day how she planned to be on fire for Jesus from then on.

A Prayer I recognise, Lord, that lukewarm Christians are only of limited use in your plans for this world. I repent before you if this is how I am. Move in my life by your Spirit so that I am on fire for you. Then work in my husband, I pray.

A Question to Answer Have you ever thought about how Jesus must feel when those for whom he died gradually start to fall out of love with him and stray away?

Coping With The Trial

Do not be surprised at the painful trial you are suffering (1 Peter 4:12)

Read: 1 Peter 4:12-19

It took a Sunday evening sermon that she did not want to hear to show Valerie that God had not abandoned her. Her weekend had been fraught with tension. She had struggled to cope with two of her children who were ill, then in the morning she had been stopped from attending church because her husband had insisted on playing golf. He arrived home quite late in the afternoon. By then, she was already feeling tense and totally unprepared to go to church that evening, but he insisted she should go. She went, but only to get some peace and quiet.

However, during the previous few weeks, Valerie had been feeling increasingly unhappy at her domestic situation. Her husband was always making fun of her church and faith. She felt it was so unfair, as she did nothing knowingly to provoke him. One evening he was extremely sarcastic about both in front of their dinner guests, who were Valerie's friends from work, and she became especially angry.

The sermon in church that night focused on Jesus' death on the cross and how, humanly, his immense sacrifice was totally unjust. Valerie began to see her situation differently as the sermon progressed. She was having to endure a trial – but a much less serious one than Jesus went through for her. By the time the sermon ended she saw that it was a privilege for any Christian to 'participate in the sufferings of Christ' (1 Pet 4:13), and she went home with a new attitude and commitment.

A Prayer Help me to see my trials in perspective, Lord, rather than becoming miserable when life gets hard. Show me how you could work positively in my husband's life.

A Practical Suggestion In the next few days try to visit someone you know, maybe from your church, who is having a hard time too. Ask God to let your visit be a great encouragement to them.

A Reunited Family

His heart went out to her (Luke 7:13)

Read: Luke 7:11-17

Gillian had been married to Ron, her second husband, for two years. She had been widowed five years before when Jim had died suddenly from a heart attack. He was a dedicated Christian and they, together with their three children, had been a genuinely happy family. However, the impact of his death had affected Gillian deeply, and she found that her faith began to slide as she gradually came to terms with what had happened.

It was while she was struggling to understand how a loving God could deprive her of her husband that she met Ron and fell in love. When they had been married for a while it began to dawn on Gillian what she was missing. Ron had only a loose interest in Christianity, and as she recognised that their relationship lacked any spiritual dimension, she began to feel disillusioned.

When Jesus saw the effects of cruel separation as he entered Nain, he felt compassion for the mother whose only son had died. However, Jesus did not merely empathise or attempt to console her. He used his extraordinary power to reunite the family as he raised the boy from the dead.

Jesus' heart goes out to Gillian too. He understands her pain – both over Jim's death and the lack of a spiritual relationship with Ron. What is more, he is committed to working with Gillian as her faith begins to grow again, and she starts to share the Good News of Jesus with Ron.

A Prayer Please help me to grasp, Lord, that when I feel pain inside, you feel it too. Thank you for the understanding and support you give me, but also for your commitment to help reduce it.

A Practical Suggestion Take some time to meditate about how Jesus perceives your current position. Ask him to reveal to you how he feels. If you sense he is sad, ask him to minister strength, hope and encouragement to you.

The Effect of Change

He received his sight and followed Jesus (Mark 10:52)

Read: Mark 10:46-52

Jennifer had been unwell for so long that she could hardly recall what it felt like to be free of pain and discomfort. Depression had overtaken her at times, but the first sign of encouragement came when her neighbour, Teresa, invited her to a healing meeting at a nearby church. Jennifer had never thought about an answer to her problems lying anywhere other than in conventional medicine, but she was both desperate and intrigued, and joined Teresa with an open mind. She was impressed by what she heard and, displaying small but genuine faith in God, went forward to be prayed for. The miracle was not instant, but over the next few days her pain grew less, her spirits lifted, and within a week she was like a different person. Everyone who met her remarked on the transformation, not least her husband Bill.

He had been highly sceptical of all faith and religion until then, but he could not deny the change in Jennifer's health and disposition. Not surprisingly, she was enthusiastic about the God who had radically altered her life, and was keen to get to know him better. She thought Bill would feel the same way, but he was more cautious.

It is no great surprise that anyone whom Jesus heals opts to follow him, but it is always harder for those who look on, even though they may be amazed and impressed. Jennifer's role now is gently to encourage Bill, rather than condemn him because he is taking longer than her to trust Jesus.

A Prayer Please help me, Lord, to follow Jesus faithfully but not to put unreasonable pressure on my husband, which could drive him further away from you. Please give me the wisdom I need.

A Question to Answer To whatever extent Jesus has worked in your life so far, do you take time regularly to thank him for his goodness and love?

Waiting for Harvest

Yet when planted, it grows and becomes the largest of all garden plants
(Mark 4:32)

Read: Mark 4:30-34

Despite the jubilant worship in her church, Judith was discouraged one Sunday as she had coffee afterwards with some of her friends. Not many Sundays before she had heard a sermon on evangelism and sensed strongly that God was calling her to talk about him to her husband, Gerry. In the following couple of weeks she had found two or three opportunities to do so, telling him simply but coherently who Jesus is and the difference he makes to life today. She even told him how she had become a Christian herself. Now, though, she was disappointed because it seemed to have made no difference to him at all.

Jesus' parable about the mustard seed is one of his simplest and shortest, but for people like Judith it is among the most encouraging. We take it for granted in the world of nature that plants grow gradually, and it takes maybe years or decades for them to reach a substantial size. Jesus taught that the remarkable seed which is the Good News of God's kingdom, tiny and apparently insignificant though it may seem, will grow ultimately to become both enormous and influential. From Jesus' own ministry and that of his disciples it has grown into the world-wide Christian church which is now a part of virtually every nation on earth.

While we applaud Judith's desire to see Gerry become a Christian quickly, she may have to wait and pray for much longer before the seed of the Gospel germinates and grows in him. Yet it is the most important thing in all the world that she can do.

A Prayer I do not find it easy to be patient, Lord. Please keep me faithful to you and my husband until he responds to your love.

A Practical Suggestion If you share the Gospel with your husband, but can only tell him a little part at a time, make a written note of the things you say so that, by referring to your list, you can ensure that over a period you can include all the main ingredients of the Gospel.

God's Unseen Forces

Those who are with us are more than those who are with them (2 Kings 6:16)

Read: 2 Kings 6:8-23

Hannah was not pleased with her church. It was planning a mission, and while children, young people and the elderly were being targeted, Hannah's husband, Josh, and other husbands whose wives were part of the church, seemed to be ignored. Nothing at all was being arranged to reach them, so armed with a constructive list of possible ideas, Hannah visited the pastor to tell him of her concern. She felt that sports-related events could be ideal as many of the men she had in mind were firm supporters of the local soccer club, and others of them played golf and squash. Hannah's concern was that these men could be side-lined, and she felt that the church had a responsibility to invest resources in reaching them.

Elisha's servant learned an important lesson as he went out with his master one morning and saw his city surrounded by an enemy army. Not surprisingly he thought the worst, and suspected that his own, Elisha's and many other lives were in danger. At first, he could not see what Elisha saw; God had sent his own army out in force, and ultimate victory was assured.

In the same way, Hannah cannot see all the resources God has lined up in strategic positions in order that he can accomplish his will on earth. Quite apart from any investment that Hannah's church can make in reaching unbelieving husbands, without doubt, God is working independently too. However, Hannah's pastor is organising a football match!

A Prayer Thank you, Lord, for the work of your Holy Spirit, your angels, your servants on earth, and for all your investment in your work in our world. Thank you for bringing me to yourself. Now work in my husband and family too, I pray.

A Question to Answer Do you, like Elisha, trust God to work in any way he chooses in situations for which you are praying?

Counting the Cost

Will a man rob God? Yet you rob me (Malachi 3:8)

Read: Malachi 3:1-12

Geraldine usually found it a welcome relief to be able to escape from her boisterous but loveable family each Tuesday evening when she attended the house group that met near her home. There she found friendship, love, understanding and support. One day, however, she found herself struggling with a dilemma during the Bible study. She knew that with Chris, her husband, not being a practising Christian, there was no way that she could give much financially to the church. The study was about the Bible's teaching on giving, and as it progressed she felt uneasy.

She listened carefully as the leader explained that God expected the Israelites to give a tithe or a tenth of their earnings to him, together with additional offerings at other times. She heard that the New Testament principle of giving was based on God's incredible demonstration of love in sending Jesus to our world. Thankfully, the leader was kind and sensitive. He realised that for Geraldine and others this would be a delicate subject, yet he knew it was his task to explain simply and precisely what God's Word says.

It was when the meeting was over and Geraldine stood on the doorstep talking to the leader and his wife that she found peace of mind. They expressed their conviction that women in Geraldine's position cannot give a tenth of the family income because it is not theirs to give. Only if Geraldine's husband agreed could she contribute more than the occasional small gift, but she need not feel guilty. God loves her and completely understands.

A Prayer I am looking to you for wisdom about this whole delicate area of giving, Lord. I do not want to feel guilty before my husband, or you.

A Practical Suggestion Today, to show your husband that you love him and care about him, buy something special that he likes, even if it is only a chocolate bar!

The Struggle for Purity

You have kept my word (Revelation 3:8)

Read: Revelation 3:7-13

Janice felt that she was under dreadful pressure. Jack, her husband of over twenty years, thought it was funny when their fourteen year-old daughter, Chloe, came home drunk from a friend's party. Janice was appalled, both that the parents of Chloe's friend had provided alcohol for youngsters of that age, and that Jack had laughed as Chloe had staggered home complaining of how ill she felt. Apart from anything else, Janice felt that as the sole Christian parent in her home she had a duty to maintain God's standards where she could.

When Jesus spoke to the church in Philadelphia he identified the huge gulf that exists between those who live according to the ways of the world and sometimes under the direct influence of Satan, and those who are determined to live for God. Inevitably, when darkness and light are in close proximity to one other, there is tension and conflict, and it is no surprise that Jesus refers to 'the hour of trial' (v10) that his followers have to endure.

There is no easy answer for Janice. For the time being she is caught between two worlds and two lifestyles. If she was to join Jack and treat Chloe's drunken state merely as a joke, she would know inside that she was failing in her duty to God as a Christian parent. On the other hand, if Janice was critical and judgmental of Chloe, her friend's parents and Jack, she could find herself alienated within her own family. Janice needs great wisdom from God so that she can remain faithful to him while trying to keep relationships intact within the family.

A Prayer Please especially help me, Lord, when I feel the tension between the lifestyle you call me to live and to teach my children, and the lifestyles of the world in which I live.

A Practical Suggestion When faced with complex situations where you feel you cannot win, do not struggle alone to work out what to do. Meet a close Christian friend and prayerfully chew the problem over with them. It will help a lot.

Being Responsible Stewards

You have been faithful with a few things (Matthew 25:21)

Read: Matthew 25:14-30

Hazel had been suspicious for months. Since she and Bob married, he had always taken care of the family's finances. All she did was to glance at the bank statement when it arrived. What first caught her eye was that after years of financial stability, their account was now usually in the red. When she asked Bob about this, he told her that prices were rising faster than their income, and there was nothing to worry about.

It was when Hazel noticed that Bob seemed keen to intercept the bank statements before she saw them that she began seriously to worry. She knew she had good cause to do so when, having found them, she discovered that for months they had been living on a bank overdraft, although she could not see why their living expenses had risen. As a Christian she believed God would meet the family's needs, a conviction Bob did not share. Hazel believed in using responsibly what God entrusted to them, and she was grateful that her husband, though not a Christian, generally agreed that this was wise.

When Hazel confronted him, Bob confessed that he had a growing gambling habit. He could not explain why, but thought it was to bring back some excitement into his life. After releasing her anger and disappointment, Hazel promised to support Bob in breaking his addiction. They decided to strive together to restore the family's finances to the point where Hazel sensed once again that they were acting as good stewards of what God had given them.

A Prayer Please give me patience and determination to counteract problems in my life that make me feel uneasy before you, Lord, while also helping me to be sensitive to my husband.

A Question to Answer Think...are there any problems relating to your marriage that you are not facing up to at the moment? If so, consider how you can tackle them rather than leaving them unattended and possibly getting worse.

The Conflict of Interests

Be holy in all you do (1 Peter 1:15)

Read: 1 Peter 1:13-25

Neither Barbie nor Jim could understand each other sometimes. Normally they got on well, but there were some occasions when Barbie wondered why he made such bizarre decisions. Similarly, Jim wondered why Barbie was sometimes so pedantic about issues that he regarded as relatively unimportant.

Their latest conflict came when Lisa, their teenage daughter, returned from school and asked if she and some friends could go out one night to the theatre in the nearby city. Both her parents agreed, not only that she could, but also when, with whom and to which play. Five weeks later and the day before the trip, Barbie learned from a friend that the play included both nudity and strong language and immediately she considered it was unsuitable for Lisa to see. Barbie was definite that Lisa must not go. After all, as a Christian, Barbie was trying to eliminate from her own life, and the lives of her children, those evil influences that corrupt and destroy. Jim, a nominal Christian, argued that Lisa was exposed to them at school far more than her mother realised, and that as the evening at the theatre had been booked for weeks, Lisa should be allowed to go.

Lisa did go, but Barbie prayed extra hard for her, expressing to God her regret that she had agreed so quickly to the trip in the first place. God gave her peace, and slowly she began to feel that he at least respected her desire for holiness.

A Prayer When I get drawn into situations that catch me unawares, please reassure me, Lord, that you understand my dilemma and forgive my naivety.

A Practical Suggestion Try to think and plan ahead so as to avert at an early stage situations which could give you problems later.

The Power of the Gospel

The Lord opened her heart to respond (Acts 16:14)

Read: Acts 16:11-15

It was seven years since Julie Ann had become a Christian. She had been to a big evangelistic meeting organised by a local church, heard the gospel for the first time and was attracted to the positive message of security and reassurance that the preacher had presented. Within two weeks she had made a commitment to Jesus Christ but, because she knew that Frank, her husband, had no religious background, she played down what had happened to her. She went to church most Sundays, but she never really gave Frank any explanation of the spiritual change that had taken place deep inside her.

Now, seven years on, Frank had stopped worrying about what his wife had got into. He had to admit that, if anything, Julie Ann was easier to live with than before, and her friends from church seemed genuine and sincere. He simply perceived her faith as something that suited her, but it never occurred to him that it could be for him too. That was until one Christmas Eve when, for the first time, Julie Ann asked Frank to go to church with her. He said he would, and there he heard the same gospel his wife had responded to earlier. It struck a chord in him and within a month he too became a follower of Jesus.

The first question he asked Julie Ann was, 'Why didn't you tell me about this before?' Like the presentation of the gospel to Lydia and her household, this one also bore rapid fruit.

A Prayer Give me wisdom, please Lord, to know when and how to share the Good News of Jesus with my husband and others close to me who do not believe yet.

A Practical Suggestion Prepare, both in your mind and in writing, how you will begin and continue a presentation of the gospel to your partner when God gives you opportunities to share it with him.

At a Distance

I have not found such great faith even in Israel (Luke 7:9)

Read: Luke 7:1-10

Times had been troubled for so long for Lyn and Roger that they had agreed to a trial separation. As the years had passed, both of them had opted to pursue their separate interests. This meant that at different times each of them left the children with their partner, as one or the other went out. However, it was Lyn's faith in Jesus Christ which probably caused most disruption because, having become a Christian and joined a church, she could attend numerous activities throughout the week. She tried to be wise as to how many she went to, but Roger frequently told her it was too many.

Now that Roger had been gone from the family home for a couple of months and only called at the house to take the children out, Lyn had time to think and pray. As she reflected, she saw how each of them had drifted from the other, and how they had become increasingly distant. This made a crisis of some kind almost inevitable. She also recognised that having become a Christian there were two important things she had not done. First, she had never really explained her new faith to Roger so that he understood what had happened to her and why she wanted to go to church. Secondly, she had never told him the gospel so that he had a chance to respond to Jesus Christ too.

Following repentance, Lyn prayed earnestly for Roger in a way she had never done before. She believed that if distance did not prevent Jesus from working in the centurion's servant, nothing need hinder him from working in Roger's life either.

A Prayer Give me the faith, I ask you, Lord, to be able to pray for those who are distant from you. Please answer my prayer and work in their lives.

A Question to Answer Have you imagined your partner or someone close to you who does not know the Lord yet becoming a Christian? Pray for this to happen!

Partnership With God

The Lord routed Sisera (Judges 4:15)

Read: Judges 4:4-16

Josie was uncertain what to do next. She knew that when she and Richard married they had both been thinking about faith. They had spent a lot of time together reading and asking their friends and colleagues what they had discovered and experienced. Since then Josie had gone one way and become a committed Christian, while Richard had decided not to adhere to any faith but just to remain 'open to them all'. Josie saw his decision as pure evasion.

This state of affairs had lasted for several years when Josie heard a sermon at church one Sunday that struck her forcibly. The pastor reminded the congregation that God wants to work in the lives of all those people who come within our circle of relationships, especially those who live with us. However, God's way is not to work independently of us, nor to leave us alone to accomplish his work, but for us to work in a remarkable partnership with him.

This was how the Israelites achieved a notable victory over Sisera under the leadership of the prophetess, Deborah, and Barak, the commander of the army. Deborah knew in advance that the Lord had gone ahead of his people and victory was assured. Then it happened. Barak and his ten thousand men took an active part in the victory and yet, when it came, it was attributed to God. Now Josie has committed herself to work in partnership with God so that, as he works, Richard can become one of his family too.

A Prayer Please help me, Lord, to be prepared to let go of my own plans so that I can work in close co-operation with you to see my family and friends brought to faith in Jesus.

A Practical Suggestion As well as praying for your husband to come to faith in Jesus, talk and pray through with a friend how God can use you best so that he and you co-operate fully together.

Seeing Through the Lies

The serpent was more crafty… (Genesis 3:1)

Read: Genesis 3:1-19

Joan and Paul were exhausted as they entered the counselling centre one morning. They had talked and argued for much of the night and, even when they stopped, neither of them had slept. This morning they were due to see their counsellor for the fourth time, having been asked to prepare by talking about any interests they had in common. Their discussion had covered the sports and recreational interests which had drawn them together in the first place, and they had debated this fairly amicably. However, it was their respective families, together with Joan's new-found faith, which were the main areas of conflict.

The counsellor's non-directive approach was aimed at helping Joan and Paul to work out where they thought their relationship was going. She acted simply as a facilitator, but, sadly, as they talked with her, their mood was so negative that neither of them saw much prospect ahead of any stable relationship.

Adam and Eve ate the forbidden fruit in Eden because Satan deceived them both. Today he still likes tricking people into thinking they have freedom to decide whatever they like irrespective of God's desires. Before deciding the future, Joan especially needs to realise that God has declared marriage to be a permanent uniting of two people. Also, now that she believes in Jesus, Joan's relationship with Paul gives him an opportunity to discover God's love through his Christian wife. If both of them could commit themselves to working at their relationship, and Joan can draw on God's loving resources, there is hope yet!

A Prayer When I see our marriage from a purely human perspective, help me, Lord, to see things from your angle. Then give me hope and a capacity to trust you.

A Question to Answer Can you think of any reasons why your marriage might not prosper in the future? What do you think God may be saying to you about these areas?

Hearing God Anywhere

God gave knowledge and understanding (Daniel 1:17)

Read: Daniel 1:1-21

Jodie never travelled far during childhood, and it therefore came as a huge shock when, just four years after she married Tom, his company transferred him to take charge of a department in one of their offices in the Middle East. Jodi's other big surprise in the early days of her marriage was how God called her into a relationship with himself. This was a shock because her family had always frowned on anything to do with religion, but through a neighbour Jodie had heard about Jesus and had responded to his love.

Now Jodie found herself in an alien country surrounded by an unusual culture and a religion she found very hard to understand. She was separated from her family by a huge distance but, like Daniel in Babylon, she found spiritual fellowship in this foreign setting as she met for worship, study and prayer with other expatriate Christian wives. Together they prayed for husbands like Tom who had not yet come to Christ, and found that God encouraged them as they spent time with him.

What thrilled Jodie most was that even here, far from home, God was caring for her and helping her faith to grow. It could have been so different, and she could have felt isolated and even given up her faith altogether. As it was she missed her family badly, but being happily married and spending time with her Christian friends, she was able to keep trusting God. As for Tom, she prayed increasingly that he would discover Jesus' love for himself.

A Prayer Help me to trust you, Lord, especially if I am away from familiar surroundings, family and friends. I pray too that my husband will be more open to you away from home.

A Practical Suggestion Phone someone today who may be far from where you now live, but who you know will support you and your husband in prayer if you ask. Alternatively, you could write to them.

Being Understood

How can I give you up? (Hosea 11:8)

Read: Hosea 11:1-11

Tiffany was so grateful to know that God understood how she felt. Her sadness was nothing new, but it seemed to hit her harder than usual one weekend. She and Derek had been together for over ten years. Tiffany had only married him after a well-meaning friend had told her what she wanted to hear, that it did not matter that she was a Christian and he was not. If she remained committed to God, she was told, there was nothing to worry about, and Derek would be a believer within a year or two. In the event, Tiffany had to learn the hard way that things do not necessarily happen as conveniently as we would like.

Now, some years later, after hearing a sermon at church on the pain God feels, Tiffany was feeling disappointed, yet reassured. She knew herself well enough to know that she had a tendency to feel sorry for herself when things do not go her way, but this was different. Her sadness was caused by her lack of spiritual unity with Derek, and her incapacity to be able to share anything to do with her faith with him.

Hosea 11 is an eloquent reminder that pain is not an alien emotion to the heart of God. He feels great pangs of disappointment and regret when his chosen people, whether Jews or contemporary Christians, go their own way, forget who has sustained them, and put other things or people in his place. Tiffany was reassured that God knew of her pain, and that he was sad, too, that so far Derek had not responded to his love.

A Prayer Please console me when I need it, Lord, and give me the patience and love to be able to handle disappointment like you.

A Question to Answer Are you sure you are doing all you can, in co-operation with God, to help what you are praying for to happen?

80

Keeping Pure

The body is not meant for sexual immorality (1 Corinthians 6:13)

Read: 1 Corinthians 6:12-20

It happened only rarely but, when an attractive man paid Judy a compliment, it made her knees turn to jelly. It had been like this since she was a teenager and nice-looking boys at school had acted playfully with her. Even now she was older it had the same effect, despite the fact that she was married to Jon and had three children.

It was a casual comment by a man at the office about how nice she looked that began Judy's journey to near-disaster. Allan was almost certainly testing her out to see how she responded, but it was hardly any time at all before they began flirting each time they met in the corridor. Then they began to meet after work, telling their respective partners that they were working late. It was not long before their relationship became adulterous, and while Judy, a Christian for a few years, knew it was thoroughly wrong, the excitement and sense of danger made her block out God's voice completely.

Only several months later did Judy see things differently. Despite the hypocrisy, she had continued to take her children to church, and one Sunday the minister preached about adultery, explaining all the reasons why God perceives it as a sin. For the next few days Judy lived in a state of confusion, with her mind and emotions pulling in different directions. Her eventual desperation drove her to a Christian friend, and after talking and praying, Judy stopped her sinful relationship, rededicated herself to God and resolved once again to let him use her to help bring her husband to Christ.

A Prayer Please help me to see my sin as you see it, Lord, and to understand that if I repent of any sin, you will forgive me.

A Practical Suggestion Identify something in your life that you know Jesus would never do, think or say.

Receiving Guidance

The Spirit of Jesus would not allow them (Acts 16:7)

Read: Acts 16:6-10

Having believed in Jesus for some years, Pat was especially keen for her husband, Frank, to come to faith in Jesus too. Soon after her conversion she had decided that she would only pressurise Frank to join her at church at Christmas and Easter. She hoped that if she was relaxed about church for the rest of the year, sometimes he would choose to accompany her of his own accord.

Sadly, however, Frank had never opted to do this, and, indeed, had often been reluctant to join Pat for seasonal celebrations, especially Easter. One day it dawned on Pat that Frank was making no headway at all and that if they were not careful, nothing about this would ever change. This concerned her greatly, and made her start praying for some fresh insight and direction from the Lord.

While Paul and his colleagues were pioneer missionaries, God guided them from place to place, sometimes surprising them by closing doors as well as opening others. Whenever any of us senses God is uneasy about a particular course of action, we need to take time to reassess, pray and ask him to show us what to do next and when. As we see how God used Paul in Macedonia, it is clear that it was his divine plan for Paul and his friends to go there. Similarly, Pat needs to know the new strategy God wants her to use at home with Frank.

A Prayer Help me to recognise, Lord, if there are areas of my life that need fresh direction or emphasis. Speak clearly to me.

A Practical Suggestion Arrange to meet a close Christian friend, or maybe your Pastor, to evaluate and pray through your strategy for helping your husband to find Jesus Christ personally. Ask God to help you to have an open mind.

The Ultimate Question

Ask for whatever you want me to give you (2 Chronicles 1:7)

Read: 2 Chronicles 1:1-12

Ann knew that her prayers were sometimes restricted. You only had to say the word 'prayer' in her presence and she would tell you how she was asking God for Jim, her husband, to become a Christian. When an opportunity was given in church or a small group meeting for open prayer, Ann was usually one of the first to participate, and everyone in the church knew the main thing she would ask for from God. They admired her perseverance, but felt her prayers were somewhat repetitive.

King Solomon was given one of the greatest privileges of all time when God invited him to ask for anything at all. His choice of 'wisdom and knowledge' (v10) was essentially not for himself, but so that he could 'lead' and 'govern' God's people effectively as king. Solomon ensured that his main request to the Lord was for something that would benefit God's work and the lives of others more than himself.

One day, one of Ann's friends plucked up courage and suggested that there must be other things that Ann could pray for. She also enquired why Ann's prayers were preoccupied with Jim. She found out that Ann was so fed up with the rows at home because of her faith that she thought her husband's conversion would be the quickest and easiest way to obtain peace. Once Ann recognised that her main motive was selfish, she rethought her prayer strategy. She kept praying for Jim, although mainly in private, and the church breathed a sigh of relief!

A Prayer Please help me to understand, Lord, if any of my prayers are essentially selfish. If so, show me, so that like Solomon I can ask you primarily for things that will benefit others and bring glory to you.

A Practical Suggestion Pray your prayers today as you usually do. Afterwards, list what you prayed for, then analyse why you asked God for each thing. Return to the list in the coming days and note which prayers have been answered.

Expressing Love

How beautiful you are, my darling! (Song of Songs 4:1)

Read: Song of Songs 4:1-15

Denise was becoming increasingly frustrated by the way her husband seemed to take less and less interest in her. Before they were married he was more romantic than any man she had ever met, and he treated her with great respect and courtesy. He often bought her flowers and other gifts, but now, almost three months into their marriage, he was different, and seemed far less romantically inclined. Denise wondered if their relationship was disintegrating, and under the surface was anxious as well as frustrated.

The romance expressed by the lovers in the Song of Songs shows how wholesome and enriching human love can be. This is one of God's gifts to the human race, and this passage describes what Denise thought was the essence of her relationship with Tom. However, what she did not know was that Tom had not realised that there was any change between them, nor did he feel that he loved his wife less than before.

This highlights the difference sometimes evident between the sexes. Whereas intimacy and romance are important to women, men are less adept at using words to communicate, especially when it comes to expressions of intimacy. As a newly-married man, Tom had unconsciously adopted what he considered to be the role of a husband. He needed gentle encouragement from Denise to see that the romance they had both incorporated into their courtship needed to be an important element in their marriage too.

A Prayer Please show me how best I can encourage my husband to include romance and intimacy in our relationship if I sense it is missing.

A Practical Suggestion Make your husband his favourite meal tonight, and serve it in as intimate setting as you can.

Being Role Models

Nobody should seek his own good, but the good of others
(1 Corinthians 10:24)

Read: 1 Corinthians 10:23 - 11:1

Wilf felt that he had to express his disappointment to his wife, Jane. A group from her church had been to the house for an evening meeting and, while Wilf had not been part of it, he had inadvertently heard some of the discussion while he brought in the coffee. He had been alarmed to hear a barrage of criticism about their pastor, a man whom Wilf respected from his occasional encounters with him, usually at carol services and church social events he had attended. Wilf felt let down to hear Christians speaking like this of their leader, and not only did it concern him but it also disillusioned him. He thought Christianity had a strong emphasis on love and care, and actively discouraged critical attitudes. He was right, of course. Not only was it unhelpful for church members to speak that way, but it was also an appalling witness to unbelievers like Wilf.

Paul encouraged the Christians in Corinth not to get bound up in unnecessary religious actions, especially if they might hinder other people from discovering God. It is important that everyone has the maximum opportunity to get to know God without Christians hampering them in any way. Indeed, Christians ought to be positive role models who encourage others to follow Jesus too.

Jane was acutely embarrassed when Wilf explained how he had reacted. She apologised, although she knew that damage had already been done, and she promised to tell her friends so that this would never happen again.

A Prayer Help me to be sensitive to other people, Lord, and especially never to hinder others from finding you. As far as possible, please protect my husband from anything that will stop him from encountering your love.

A Practical Suggestion Whenever you speak with other people today, try to think through how they may be responding to what you say. Are they hearing Christian attitudes?

Being Part of the Family

My mother and brothers are those who hear God's word and put it into practice (Luke 8:21)

Read: Luke 8:19-21

Compared to some of her other friends whose husbands did not share their faith, Abigail knew she had it easy. Jeremy was more co-operative than many Christian husbands when it came to helping and encouraging her in her faith. He would try to get home from work early if she asked him so that she could attend church events, and on Sundays he would prepare lunch while the family went to church. Nor did Jeremy have any problem with the children saying grace before meals or Abigail reading Bible stories to them at bedtime. The only dilemma for Abigail was that while Jeremy was wonderfully supportive of her faith, he had none of his own, and nor did he seem to be seeking it.

When Jesus was told that his relatives had come to see him, he explained that, ultimately, his family is those who not only know God's truth, but also apply it in their lives. This concerned Abigail. She knew that while Jeremy agreed with the essence of Christian teaching, he had made no personal commitment to accept it for himself and to live a Christian lifestyle. The saddest thing for Abigail was that Jeremy was so near to God's kingdom, and yet so far away.

People like Jeremy need a lot of spiritual investment. Their position is akin to sitting on a fence, and something has to happen before they are ever likely to seriously re-evaluate it. So often a person sees no need to change, because their life is fairly comfortable. In this situation, Abigail needs to keep praying...

A Prayer Where I know someone who needs fresh insight into spiritual things, Lord, show me how I can best pray and serve both them and you. Please draw them into your family.

A Question to Answer Have you resolved to live as closely as you can to the teaching of God's word in every area of your life?

Explaining Your Position

Always be prepared to give an answer (1 Peter 3:15)

Read: 1 Peter 3:8-22

The evenings were often the most traumatic times in Georgie and Malcolm's home, and the television was often at the centre of their disagreements. Their son, Andy, aged fifteen, often wanted to watch the same programmes as his dad, but if Georgie was uneasy about her husband watching programmes with gratuitous sex and violence, she was thoroughly opposed to Andy seeing them. However, Malcolm had no problem about it, believing that Andy needed exposure to the real world. He spoke with disdain of Georgie and her church friends who seemed, in his view, to restrict their TV viewing to programmes that lacked any character or excitement.

Georgie found this hard to handle and learned that there was no way she could keep Andy from watching TV with his father. All she could do (and often she felt guilty because she thought it was inadequate) was to try to talk to Andy about what he saw, explaining simply and honestly how she felt about it and why.

Being ready to explain why is important for every believer. This applies to every situation – whether faced with unbelievers who question what Christians believe, or finding the need to explain why you live the kind of lifestyle you do. On the whole, others will show at least some respect for those whose choices are different to their own if they can explain the principles behind them. Georgie's prayer is that as she tries to do this, both Andy and Malcolm will hear what she says and be affected positively by it.

A Prayer Help me, Lord, to be able to think clearly and express my faith succinctly when there are opportunities to do so. When I share with my husband, help him to listen and understand.

A Practical Suggestion If people you live with misunderstand any part of your Christian faith, try to work out why. Then, when the time is right, explain your position to them.

Coping With Offence

An offended brother is more unyielding than a fortified city (Proverbs 18:19)

Read: Proverbs 18:1-20

Jason and Melissa were genuinely concerned that Jerry, their seventeen year-old son, was heading for trouble. He was rude, offensive and uncommunicative, and he irritated his mother in particular by treating his home like a hotel and expecting everyone to clear up after him. He also spent much of his time with a group of friends who seemed even more rough and uncouth than he was. Jason and Melissa sensed that at any time Jerry could get into trouble with the law, and even face the prospect of a prison sentence.

As they talked about their fears, they began to realise that they might have contributed to the negative attitude Jerry now seemed to have towards them. During much of his formative years his parents had been at loggerheads because Jason had reacted so strongly to Melissa becoming a Christian soon after their son's birth. Jerry had arrived prematurely, and it was only skilled nursing and prayer that ensured his survival. In her distress, Melissa had turned to God. She found that he became so real to her that, from then on, her life had to centre on him. Jason resented this, and Jerry grew up among frequent arguments, mainly about when Melissa could and could not go to church.

As they saw that their parenting had been deficient and that Jerry was probably now rebelling against the atmosphere in which he grew up, Jason and Melissa agreed to talk with Jerry together and to apologise. They sensed it could do no harm, and that it might help to repair the broken relationships.

A Prayer Please help my husband and I to see clearly any mistakes we have made in our parenting which may be rebounding on us today. Then give us the grace and humility to apologise if that seems appropriate.

A Practical Suggestion Think back to specific days and events that you recall spending with your children, maybe as a family. Relive one or two in your imagination, and evaluate what it must have been like to have your husband and yourself as parents.

A Constant Supply

The jug of oil did not run dry (1 Kings 17:16)

Read: 1 Kings 17:7-24

Jodie had had a tough time at home for many years. She and Dave, her husband, certainly loved each other, but he really could not understand why, some years before, she had become a Christian. He did not appreciate all the phone calls from her church friends whom he did not know, nor was he keen that a weekly housegroup met in their home one lunchtime each week. He felt excluded from this area of her life, which she obviously enjoyed, and sometimes his frustration and disappointment came to the surface.

Jodie found that she coped with the tension best when she prayed more and took extra time to share her feelings openly and honestly with God. She did not understand what happened, but found that as she told God of her need, somehow he strengthened and encouraged her so that she could carry on. In Elijah's day too, God proved his love and faithfulness to a woman and her family by miraculously supplying resources that they needed desperately.

God's remarkable capacity of knowing precisely what our needs are, and then being able to meet them, is highly reassuring as we face up to each day's tensions and problems. As the Apostle Paul found, God does not tend to remove those things with which we struggle; rather he gives us special grace and power to rise above them (2 Cor 12:7-10). Jodie's experience is that God has never let her down even though, sometimes, life at home is not easy.

A Prayer Help me to trust you, Lord, especially when things at home are demanding and I feel out of my depth. Please stand close beside me, and pour out your grace and strength into my life.

A Practical Suggestion Work through one of the Gospels and count how many times Jesus came to the rescue of his disciples when they were struggling and getting out of their depth.

On the Hot Spot

Just say whatever is given you at the time (Mark 13:11)

Read: Mark 13:1-13

Janine was fuming by the time she arrived home. She had expected that she and her husband, Robert, would enjoy a quiet and relaxed evening with some mutual friends. However, during the meal Robert began to make fun of the fact that Janine had recently begun attending church, and their friends soon joined in. In fact, all three of them turned on Janine who felt both overwhelmed and threatened by the rather harsh and intimidating questions they posed. Having been a Christian for only a few weeks, she struggled with some of her answers, and she sensed that she let the Lord down by her hesitant replies. When they got indoors, Janine told Robert exactly how she felt for having started this off.

While training his disciples, Jesus ensured that he prepared them as fully as possible for the persecution they may experience if they aimed to remain loyal to him. Physical punishment and judicial proceedings would be among the painful experiences they would have to endure. Later, of course, he himself had to cope with all this—and more, as he suffered for the sins of the world.

Although Janine's experience did not take place in a courtroom, she was certainly interrogated about her faith by those who intended to make her look foolish if they could. Yet God was with her through this ordeal as he promises to be when his children are put on the spot for their faith. Indeed, Robert found Janine's simple but honest answers full of such conviction that he quickly apologised and promised never to do this to her again.

A Prayer Please be close to me and guide me whenever I am called to give account of my faith, Lord. Give me the ability to trust you in these demanding times.

A Practical Suggestion Write down your testimony of how you first became a Christian. Then try to memorise it so that you can tell anyone who specifically asks you for an explanation.

Giving Positive Support

Accept one another, then, just as Christ accepted you (Romans 15:7)

Read: Romans 15:1-13

Janey was unbelievably ecstatic when, after several weeks of encouragement, her husband agreed to go with her to her church's carol service.
This was her first Christmas as a Christian, and she had been looking
for opportunities to invite Mike to join her at an event where the
gospel would be explained. She was so keen for them to be united in
the Christian faith, that before the day, she prayed so hard that once
Mike got there, he would enjoy it.

It was what happened after the service, together with the events of
the next couple of weeks, that caused Janey's ecstasy to turn to pain.
She was disappointed after the carol event because hardly anyone from
the church greeted Mike or talked to him. Then, when she went to
church on Sundays over the next few weeks, Janey was met with a barrage of questions, mainly enquiring whether Mike had become a
Christian at Christmas? She sensed that no one was very interested in
Mike as a person, and she felt that this could only hinder his progress
towards the Kingdom of God.

Soon afterwards, Janey decided to pluck up courage and to go and
tell her minister of her disappointment. He listened sympathetically and,
while agreeing to her request for confidentiality, said he would talk with
the church about the need to be sensitive and to support lone Christian
wives more in various ways. He said that the church must not make it
more difficult for these wives to encourage their husbands to become
Christians.

A Prayer Please use me in any way you can, Lord, to show others in
my church the kind of support and encouragement I and other lone
Christian wives need.

A Question to Answer Have you given any support and encouragement recently to another wife whose domestic circumstances bear a
resemblance to your own?

Expressing Devotion

Mary took about a pint of pure nard..., she poured it on Jesus' feet (John 12:3)

Read: John 12:1-8

Before she became a Christian, Mariah had had an affair with a neighbour, something that affected her husband very deeply. After that he found it very difficult to trust his wife with other men, and easily became suspicious and jealous because he expected the worst. Initially, he did not see any problem when Mariah told him that she had become a Christian, but, as time went on, he began to sense that her faith was taking over her life. Alarm bells started to ring, and he tried to discourage her from going to church as often as she did.

For Mariah, committing her life to Jesus was a wonderful experience. She loved him very much because of all he had done for her, not least the forgiveness he had freely given to her for her past indiscretion. In no time at all Mariah's friends knew what had happened to her. Her newfound faith bubbled from within her and she was a radiant witness to Jesus.

Jesus never complains when his friends express their love and commitment to him. Having said that, it is not a complete surprise, given the circumstances, why Mariah's husband finds any man a threat – even Jesus! This couple probably needs outside help in order that this painful past episode can be worked through and resolved. Then, and only then, will Mariah find that she can express her passion for Jesus without fear of her husband misunderstanding.

A Prayer Please give my husband and me the courage we need to work through any past hurts that still exist and which threaten to disrupt our lives now and in the future.

A Question to Answer How many past hurts and grievances are still alive and reside in rarely opened cupboards in your marriage, ready to pounce out when you least expect them? If you discern any, try to resolve the issues with your husband now while the problem is not a bone of contention.

Standing Out From The Crowd

It is God's will that you should be holy (1 Thessalonians 4:3)

Read: 1 Thessalonians 4:1-12

Jessica had always known that her husband, Bryan, could be pretty vulgar. She saw traces of it at home sometimes, but it was primarily when he was with his mates at the pub that it was most obvious. Jessica had always tried not to go with him, but latterly, since becoming a Christian, she resisted his pressure more fiercely than ever. She had always felt embarrassed, but now she found that what he said, and the way he said it, was both crude and offensive. If she was with him in that environment now, she kept very quiet and spent her time silently asking God to protect and strengthen her.

In many of the letters in the New Testament there is strong encouragement to live a holy lifestyle that makes God's children stand out from the crowd. Jessica knew this and, secretly, she envied her female Christian friends whose husbands also had a personal faith. She felt that they were highly unlikely to have to cope with the kind of pressure that she was under. Jessica's dream was that was one day Bryan would have a Damascus road experience of Jesus, and that overnight he would become a totally reformed character.

In the meantime Jessica has to look to God for his strength because she has a delicate balancing act to do. While God still calls her to live a holy life, she knows she must not alienate Bryan or destroy the relationship they have. After all, she married him 'for better, for worse', and now, as she keeps praying for him she must give him her support, but without compromising herself before God.

A Prayer Please be especially close to me, Lord, when I find myself pulled in different directions. I am so glad you understand the pressure I am under. Help me to love and support my husband despite this.

A Practical Suggestion If your husband likes to go out to drink, try to find somewhere that you can visit together sometimes where you feel comfortable.

Showing the Grace of God

Not seven times, but seventy-seven times (Matthew 18:22)

Read: Matthew 18:21-35

Only after she married him did Camille discover what she considered to be a perverse tendency in Ryan. For some unknown reason he seemed to relish people making mistakes. Invariably, he then responded by mocking them, although rarely to their faces, although he had no reservation about doing so to Camille. When she became a Christian his expectations for her rose, and consequently she had to tolerate his mocking on a regular basis at home. She did not find it easy to cope with this, but tried to be patient.

However, things deteriorated when Camille's church ran into trouble over one specific issue which led to a near half-and-half split of the congregation. Unfortunately, Ryan worked with the husband of another woman who attended the church, and found out about this. He also discovered that she and Camille had opposing points of view, which made the situation at home more difficult for Camille. Ryan came home some nights appearing to relish the fact that he knew more sordid details of the church's bitter split, and he taunted Camille with what he knew until she began to dread his return from work.

Camille discussed the problem with one of her close friends who advised her strongly not to get drawn into discussion about this problem. She also said that Camille should ask God constantly for the capacity to be able to forgive Ryan. Harbouring resentment and bitterness would only hamper her own spiritual growth and relationship with the Lord.

A Prayer As you constantly forgive me when I ask you, Lord, please give me the same capacity to forgive my husband or anyone else who makes my life more difficult.

A Question to Answer When did you last meditate on all that Jesus went through to secure forgiveness for you? Try it!

A Big Turnaround

God changed Saul's heart (1 Samuel 10:9)

Read: 1 Samuel 10:1-16

Sophie was only too well aware of what God had done for her. Only two years earlier she was drinking heavily and finding it hard to hold her life together. She had a demanding job and was making steady progress in her career, but the increasing pressure on her to perform ever more successfully was taking its toll. The lunchtime drinks sustained her during the afternoon while most evenings were spent in a bar. Mercifully for her marriage, her husband liked to drink too.

One day the stark reality of Sophie's situation hit her and she turned to a friend for help. Katherine worked with Sophie and was the wife of the pastor of a nearby church. As they talked, Katherine told Sophie about God's love and the opportunity for a relationship with him through faith in Jesus Christ. After many months of searching, Sophie gave her life to Jesus. She stopped drinking excessively and, with Katherine's encouragement and support, she began to grow spiritually. Sophie's main concern now is for Graham, her husband, who has noticed the change in her, but so far has resisted the opportunity to discover more about God for himself.

When someone becomes open to what God can do for them, he can start to work in them. Saul made himself available for God's will to be done in his life as he listened to Samuel's prophetic words, and God changed him from the inside. As Sophie continues to pray for Graham, he could be next!

A Prayer I praise you, Lord, that you can and do work deeply in people's lives to change them. Thank you for what you have done for me. Work in those close to me, and help me to pray faithfully until they respond.

A Practical Suggestion In order to encourage your faith in God to grow, go to a Christian bookshop and choose a biography about someone whose life God has changed in a wonderful way.

Facing Tough Questions

I also want women to dress modestly (1 Timothy 2:9)

Read: 1 Timothy 2:8-15

George had been brought up by Christian parents and so had a thorough grounding in the stories and teaching of the Bible. As a teenager, he rejected both Christianity and the church, and later met and married Lynda, whose background was completely godless. It came as a surprise to George when, after a decade together, Lynda told him that she was going to a special meeting at a nearby church where a famous Christian sportsman was speaking. He was even more shocked when she came home and said that she had become a Christian.

It was then that their problems began. The only Christian women George had ever known well were his mother and aunt. Both had dressed in dull colours and refused to wear make-up and jewellery on principle. On the basis of Paul's letter to Timothy, they had argued that they would dishonour God if they dressed in a way that drew attention to themselves. George had always struggled with this, but was now anxious that his own attractive wife would have to rethink her image.

Following a hasty talk with some new Christian friends, Lynda reassured George that while she had changed inside by trusting in Jesus Christ, she was not about to throw out her wardrobe, jewellery and make-up. God does not have a problem with Christians looking smart and bright. However, when Timothy received his letter, prostitutes were commonplace in Ephesus, and Paul saw the importance of Christian women being visibly different as a witness to God.

A Prayer Please give me wisdom when deciding what clothes and accessories to buy, Lord. I want everything about me to help other people to see you.

A Practical Suggestion Take another look through your wardrobe in case you have anything that you now feel, as a Christian, it would be inappropriate to wear.

Parenting Pain

Train children in the way they should go (Proverbs 22:6)

Read: Proverbs 22:1-9

Although a lone spiritual parent because her husband was not a Christian, Cheryl was committed to bringing up her children to follow Jesus Christ. Ever since they were babies, she had taken them to church, prayed for them and told them Bible stories at home. She believed that it was important to give them a thorough spiritual training, and her only regret was that her husband completely distanced himself from this.

Everything ran smoothly until Cheryl's eldest son, Joey, was nine. By then he had noticed that his father did not go to church and seemed to do much more interesting things at home while the rest of the family was at worship. One day Joey asked his dad if he could stay with him instead of going to church, and hearing that he could, informed his mum what he intended to do. The row between Joey's parents was one he did not forget quickly.

Cheryl criticised her husband for making it too easy for Joey to break what for him was the habit of a lifetime. She also prayed intently while gently reminding Joey of his many friends at church, and of the collection of prizes he had won, and to which he could add if he came back. Eventually, a few months later, after some of his friends had pestered him to return, Joey was back at church on Sunday mornings. Cheryl breathed a sigh of relief and said a sincere prayer of thanks to God. However, she knows that this battle is far from over.

A Prayer Please help me as a Christian parent to give a strong yet sensitive lead to my children, so that they learn about you naturally in their formative years.

A Question to Answer Is there anything else that God wants you to do to help your children learn about God and his love?

Keeping Love Alive

My lover is mine and I am his (Song of Songs 2:16)

Read: Song of Songs 2:1-17

The news that her best friend's marriage was on the verge of collapse brought Sara up with a start. She had always presumed that Naomi's relationship with John was strong and happy, but learned one day that they now found they had very little in common anymore and were going to separate on a trial basis. This made Sara think. When she and Clive married they did all kinds of sporting and outdoor pursuit activities together, but now, what with her becoming a mother and a Christian, and Clive getting promotion at work, they rarely spent much time alone together relaxing. She decided to do something about it.

Sara looked in her diary straightaway and found the next evening that both she and Clive would be free. She asked him to reserve it for a surprise occasion. She decided she would make his favourite meal and that would be accompanied by her asking him to read a selection of the love-letters he had written to her while they were courting.

Afterwards, Sara was amazed at the impact of such a simple occasion. The distance that had built up between them vanished, including, it seemed, Clive's uneasiness about Sara becoming a Christian. As they laughed and cuddled on the sofa they felt young and carefree again, and afterwards Sara thanked God for inspiring her to do something that was so beneficial for their relationship.

A Prayer Help me to listen to you and to think creatively about ways in which I can encourage my marriage to be rejuvenated.

A Practical Suggestion Create your own equivalent of Sara's special evening with her husband. Above all, make it fun!

Listening to God

After the fire came a gentle whisper (1 Kings 19:12)

Read: 1 Kings 19:1-18

Jane was never clear why Ryan's attitude to her changed. It was not that she became a Christian, because she was one, albeit backslidden, when they married. However, she was aware that there was a period some months back when she seemed to spurt forward in her spiritual growth, and God became substantially more important to her than ever before. Maybe Ryan had detected her greater desire to pray and to live a holy life.

The main change in Ryan's behaviour was the way he began to blaspheme and use language that Jane found seriously offensive. To begin with she reacted strongly, ordering him to stop, but he seemed to enjoy upsetting her and deliberately continued to do it. Jane did not know what to do but, over a period of weeks, she found that if she did not respond when he became angry and began to blaspheme, he stopped sooner than if she objected.

Jane's biggest problem at this point became her sense of guilt and shame before God. She was so unhappy that blasphemous language was being uttered in her home. Initially, this hindered her relationship with God, but a good Christian friend reminded her that at times like this she needed God more than ever. Jane committed herself to spending a little longer with God each day in Bible study and prayer. If ever there was a time when she needed to hear the reassuring whisper of God's voice, this was it.

A Prayer Please reassure and help me, Lord, when I find myself out of my depth. Let me know that you understand and will support me.

A Question to Answer Did you notice in today's Bible reading how God recommissioned Elijah, and told him to go back to continue the kind of work he was doing before?

Feeling the Loss

Jesus wept (John 11:35)

Read: John 11:1-44

Josh was hurting, but Miranda could not work out what the problem was. She kept on asking him why he had lost his usual enjoyment of life and seemed to be permanently sad. When he would not tell her she spoke to her pastor's wife but, even after talking and praying about it, they were not sure about the cause. Josh's job was secure, and nothing in his life had changed. To Miranda, her husband's change of demeanour was a mystery.

However, under the surface, Josh was struggling to cope with what Miranda had told him a few weeks before. For her, telling Joshua how much she loved Jesus Christ, now her best friend, was taking a rare opportunity to witness positively, yet she was completely unaware of his response. Inside, Josh felt pushed out and excluded within his own marriage. He was devastated that his loving wife of twelve years, and whose integrity he did not doubt for a moment, now had another man occupying her thoughts – as he saw it, another first love. He was grieving because he felt he had lost her, and yet she still lived in the same house and they shared the same bed.

When his friend Lazarus died, Jesus was deeply sad. This is the normal human reaction when anyone we love is wrenched from us. Miranda and other wives in her situation must be careful not to unsettle their husbands who, of course, are not at risk when their wives love Jesus too.

A Prayer Help me, Lord, to be gentle in how I witness to my faith in you to those who are close to me. Give me great sensitivity, I ask.

A Question to Answer Have you ever planned how you will share your faith with your husband when a spontaneous opportunity arises?

Living For God

They may be won over without words (1 Peter 3:1)

Read: 1 Peter 3:1-7

Unusually, Sharon and Tony were joined at their wedding by local newspaper reporters and a TV crew. They had grown up on the same estate, meeting first when they began nursery together. They started going out in their early teens, and their love for each other grew until, when they were nineteen, they decided to marry. The media became interested when they learned that Sharon and Tony had invited to their wedding all the youngsters who had begun nursery at the same time as them.

After they had been married for a couple of years, Sharon found herself working with a girl who was a committed Christian. Her attitude to life and her job, together with her genuine warmth and care for others, attracted Sharon to build a friendship with her. Within a few months Sharon had heard the good news of the gospel, and only a few weeks later she made a personal commitment of her life to Jesus Christ.

God worked deeply in her life from the outset, and soon Sharon was asking her friend how she could best help Tony to become a Christian too. It did not take long before Sharon realised the best way. At home, she would simply be herself and live as someone whose life had been changed by Jesus. She did not need to preach or be pushy. Tony had known her for so long that he could hardly fail to notice that she was now very different – changed from the inside out!

A Prayer Even though home can be one of the hardest places to live for you, Lord, please help me to be a strong vibrant witness in front of my family.

A Practical Suggestion See if you can find some other Christian wives in similar circumstances to yours. Then share and pray together about the way you can witness at home.

Always There

Whenever…the rainbow appears in the clouds, I will remember my covenant
(Genesis 9:14-15)

Read: Genesis 9:1-17

Louise felt generally disheartened. She was not happy in her job, her best friend had just moved away, and she felt isolated at church, largely because most other people of her age were not only married (as she was), but worshipped as couples. Louise always felt conspicuous and uneasy when she walked into church alone. She prayed regularly for Nick's conversion, but so far he had not responded at all. Overall, life was hard going and she could not see what might change to make it any easier.

Having been in church circles for some years, Louise knew that Christians sometimes suffer crises of faith, although she never had herself. That was until she found a number of things start to pile up around her and begin to overwhelm her. What concerned her most was the thought that kept flooding her mind even though she kept trying to push it away. 'Where is God in all this?' she asked, as she struggled to work out how she felt and why.

It was only as she looked out of her lounge window one evening that God spoke to her without even saying a word. Against a dark sky she saw a magnificent rainbow, and could not help but remember God's promise to Noah. As she reflected on the fact that God would be faithful whatever happened, she found her heart being warmed and her spirit coming alive. In that moment she knew that God had not abandoned her – and never would!

A Prayer I want to thank you for your faithfulness to me so far, Lord, but also, in anticipation, for your promise that whatever happens you will never leave me nor forsake me.

A Question to Answer Apart from the rainbow, what other signs has God shown you that have expressed his faithfulness to you?

Learning to Trust

Unless I see the nail marks in his hands (John 20:25)

Read: John 20:19-31

It was only after she became a Christian that Marie realised how fitting it was that her husband's name was Tom. When Marie first heard the Christian gospel she took time to reflect on her life and what Jesus had to offer, but within three months she had come to the point where she was ready to commit her life to him. Immediately she entered into a relationship with Jesus, she found it both real and meaningful.

Marie wasted no time in telling Tom about this, but he was sceptical from the start. As a scientist, he was not prepared to 'hope' that the Bible was true. His reasoning was that unless it can be proved that God exists, that Jesus is his son, and that Jesus' death and resurrection actually happened and have some kind of bearing on people today, he would dismiss it as yet another fairy tale.

Reading the Bible, Marie saw that Tom's namesake, the disciple Thomas, had problems believing in Jesus too. Despite being told of Jesus' appearance among his friends by people he would normally have trusted, Thomas could not accept that he had risen from the dead. Only when he met Jesus and saw his wounds did Thomas accept it as the truth. Marie knew that Tom would not have the privilege of an encounter like that, so she committed herself to pray that God would find another way to break through to him to bring him to faith.

A Prayer Please help trust and faith in you to grow in my husband's life. Let him recognise the reality of your new life in me.

A Question to Answer If you were accused in a court of law of being a Christian, what evidence could be presented to support the claim?

The Pain of Discipleship

Everyone will hate you because of me (Matthew 10:22)

Read: Matthew 10:1-23

From the time her children were very young, Vicki believed in the importance of reading them stories, and had accumulated a substantial pile of books by the time her fourth child was old enough to appreciate them. The Mr Men and Noddy books were some of three year-old Jane's favourites, and she asked for them every night at bedtime. Just before Jane was born, Vicki became a Christian and began reading the Bible seriously for herself. In it she discovered some remarkable and dramatic stories and it dawned on her that Jane and her older brothers would enjoy them too. Having bought a children's Bible, she started to read to them before they went to bed and they were often enthralled by what they heard.

Phil, Vicki's husband, was far from sure that this was a good idea and wasted no time in telling her so. He had grown up in a family that was very sceptical about anything religious, and he was adamant that he did not want his children indoctrinated or brainwashed. Sadly, Vicki and Phil violently disagreed about this issue many times, with neither being prepared to back down. Vicki kept reading the Bible to the children each night while Phil threatened to tear up the book and throw it away.

Jesus knew that throughout future generations people would disagree about matters of faith, and at times families would be torn apart because someone trusted in him. This does not make life any easier for Vicki, but at least she knows she is not alone in paying a high price for following Jesus.

A Prayer Having experienced the wonder of your love to me personally, Lord, I ask for your strength to persevere when it is not easy to remain faithful to you.

A Practical Suggestion Reflect on the cost Jesus paid for your forgiveness and salvation.

Responding to God's Love

Each one of you should set aside a sum of money (1 Corinthians 16:2)

Read: 1 Corinthians 16:1-9

To be honest, the sermon Paula heard in church took her by surprise. One of the reasons she had selected this particular church when she became a Christian was that it seemed to make very little reference to money. Earlier in life, Paula had attended Sunday School in a very different type of church that seemed preoccupied by its lack of money. It was always holding jumble sales, and erected a permanent thermometer outside to show the community how impoverished it was.

Paula had no doubt that the sermon her pastor preached was good and true, but it left her with a problem. She was the only Christian at home, and Terry, her husband, had only limited sympathy for her church and faith. Furthermore, he controlled the family finances, and all their money went into a joint account. What was she to do now that she had heard the pastor preach that sacrificial and proportionate giving were encouraged in the Bible? How could she possibly find more money than the pound or two that she took from the loose change in her purse each week?

As she discussed her dilemma with a friend, Paula saw that she was in a no-win situation. Terry was unlikely to agree to her giving anything much to church, and it would be devious to siphon money from their joint account without him knowing. Yet as things stood, she now felt guilty before God, so decided to pray about it until his solution became clear.

A Prayer There are issues, like money, that I struggle to know precisely what to do about, Lord. Please give me your clear guidance.

A Practical Suggestion Consider talking with your husband about how any money you earn is used in your overall budget. Would it be fair and reasonable for you to allocate some of it?

Dealing With Tension

Make every effort to live in peace (Hebrews 12:14)

Read: Hebrews 12:14-29

Neither Geoff nor Naomi could work out what was the matter with Julia, their seventeen year-old daughter. Rather unusually, they managed to have a civilised discussion about her – a rare occurrence since Geoff became severely irritated following Naomi's conversion to Christianity. He valued the weekends they spent together, and was none too pleased when she began wanting to go to church most Sundays.

For the past few months Julia had been noticeably uncommunicative at home. She told her parents virtually nothing about her studies, her feelings or her plans. They managed to extract snippets of information from her occasionally, but their once warm, friendly and out-going daughter had become ill-tempered, moody and introspective, with them at least. Geoff and Naomi were increasingly worried about her, in case she was being drawn into anything sinister that she did not want them to find out about.

Thankfully, Julia attended the church youth group, so her parents agreed that Naomi would talk discreetly to the pastor, whose home Julia often visited because she was friends with his daughter. Martin, the pastor, was reluctant to say much, but revealed that he had heard how upset Julia was that her parents often had disagreements at home. He said that she had consciously decided that she did not want to take sides, and felt that her best form of protection was to distance herself from both of them for the time being. The challenge to Geoff and Naomi was to sort out their problem before it had a long-term effect on Julia.

A Prayer I am actively committed to sorting out any unhappy personal relationships that are having a negative and destructive effect, Lord. Please help me.

A Practical Suggestion If you are in a relationship that has gone sour, determine that you will work to put it right whatever it costs and however long it takes. Try to list the first steps you could take. Is there anyone who could offer friendship and advice?

Receiving God's Strength

When you pass through the waters, I will be with you (Isaiah 43:2)

Read: Isaiah 43:1-7

Everyone has to cope with tough periods in life, but for Brenda it had lasted long enough. Her most obvious difficulty was coming to terms with her mother's death. They had always been very close, but when her mum was diagnosed as terminally ill, Brenda's life began to collapse. While she had left home two decades before, she had begun to lean on her mother for support when her own marriage began feeling cool. Her mother had been a loving and gracious source of comfort, never telling her daughter what to do but simply being in the background if she needed to talk or cry.

Her mother's death left Brenda with a big gap in her life. Sadly, it came at a time when her son's health was worrying her too. Tim was fourteen and experiencing pain in his abdomen which had his doctor baffled. He had been referred to a hospital specialist, but the appointment had not arrived by the time Brenda's mother passed away. At the funeral Brenda felt isolated and empty. Her husband, although present, seemed emotionally distant. They both knew he had never come to terms with the commitment to Jesus Christ she had made some seven years before. She appreciated him being there, but she still felt alone.

The minister who led the funeral read Isaiah 43. Brenda found the words wonderfully reassuring and sensed that God was reminding her of his personal care. While her pain and problems remained, Brenda went home knowing God was with her and that she was safe.

A Prayer When I feel alone, please come and reassure me of your love and support, Lord. Let me know you will be with me whatever happens.

A Practical Suggestion Read a Christian biography which tells how another believer has discovered God's help and strength in demanding times.

Using God's Gifts Wisely

Jonathan made David reaffirm his oath out of love for him (1 Samuel 20:17)

Read: 1 Samuel 20:1-23

Although they did not discuss it, both Jessica and Jeff knew that their relationship was not close. Their wedding had been a mere fourteen weeks after they first met, and they both knew that had they waited, they probably would never had married at all. Now, not wanting to hurt each other, they had settled into a pattern of life that provided each of them with comparative freedom.

Alarm bells began to ring in Jessica's mind a few months after she became a Christian through reading a gospel booklet she found on a train. Knowing that Christians go to church, she visited one nearby and immediately struck up a friendship with Jo, a girl of a similar age to herself. Their relationship grew as Jo discipled Jessica, encouraging her to follow Jesus and devote herself to serving him. Jessica felt so happy to be a Christian, and to have solid friendships with Jo and other Christians too.

Deep and loving friendships are part of God's gift to us. David and Jonathan were both blessed by the care and support of the other at a demanding time in their lives. However, Jessica began to see that she needed wisdom. If her relationship with Jeff was shaky before she had become a Christian, he could be edged out of her life even more now that she had allowed in both God and her new Christian friends. Jessica knew she needed God's help to try to rebuild her marriage before it was too late.

A Prayer Please help me, Lord, to be motivated to work at any important relationships in my life which have insecure foundations.

A Practical Suggestion Evaluate honestly the most important relationships in your life. Work out which are your three most important, and consider before God whether or not this order is acceptable. How could each of them be enhanced?

Commissioned to Service

Who will go for us? (Isaiah 6:8)

Read: Isaiah 6:1-10

Ten years ago Maggie became a Christian, but she knew only too well that she had not made much headway since. While to some extent she was able to play the part at church, she was aware that the attitudes her family saw at home were not very spiritual. She longed to become a more genuine Christian, but did not know how it could happen.

Then one Sunday night at church something took Maggie by surprise. Her pastor had just returned from visiting a church that had been spiritually renewed, and somehow he seemed to bring God's presence into the worship. Maggie could not easily find words to describe what happened that evening, but she found herself responding to God in a deeper way than she had ever done before. Suddenly she became aware of Jesus' rich love for her and it moved her deeply. She burst into tears, not so much of sadness although she repented of her past apathy, but of relief that Jesus had come to her and was now ministering to her hurts and disappointment.

When Maggie had responded to Jesus' love she could still feel his presence strongly. Then she found herself thinking of her husband, and sensed that God was asking her to tell him the gospel. It seemed to be a divine call to a specific task. As Isaiah had an encounter with God, so Maggie was being challenged by God to commit herself to serving him in a new way.

A Prayer Please renew my vision of you and your plan for my life. Show me especially how you can use me to show your love to my husband.

A Practical Suggestion If you know other Christians who seem to be genuinely on fire for God, try to find an opportunity to talk with them, and ask them if they can tell you how they keep close to him and in tune with his will.

A Tough Assignment

I do not know how to speak (Jeremiah 1:6)

Read: Jeremiah 1:4-19

Only very rarely was Irene lost for words, but this was one of those occasions. Through a friend at work she had been invited to a women's breakfast meeting run by a local church. It was to take place at a hotel, and a famous sports personality was going to be there to talk about her faith. Irene was keen on sport, so agreed to go.

Irene listened intently to the athlete's talk, enthralled by the stories of demanding training in all weathers, together with insights into what goes on behind the scenes in competitions. However, she found herself even more captivated by the athlete's openness as she talked of her sense of inner need and emptiness, even when competing successfully and winning awards. She told her audience how she became fulfilled only after she turned to Jesus Christ, entrusting her life and future to him. For Irene, who had long had similar feelings herself, this was highly relevant, and when an invitation was given to anyone who wanted to receive Christ, she responded.

On the way home it suddenly dawned on Irene that Barry, her husband, did not even know she had gone to a church-run meeting – let alone expect her to come home a Christian. Driving the car into her street, she prayed her first spontaneous prayer, asking God to help her to tell him. He did, just as he reassured Jeremiah when he felt inadequate. God always helps those who want to tell others about him.

A Prayer Even though it is hard, please give me the courage to tell people who are close to me, and especially my husband, that you are my Saviour and Lord.

A Practical Suggestion When you feel it is the right time to share your faith with someone, pray about the words you should use in your first sentence. Then open your mouth, speak, and trust God for what follows.

Chosen by God

Now you are the people of God (1 Peter 2:10)

Read: 1 Peter 2:4-12

Karen could not help how she felt. Keen to see her family and friends become Christians, she attended outreach training at her church. Here she learned the key elements of the Gospel, different ways to share her testimony, and how to help someone find God's love and forgiveness. The only snag was that it was now two years since the course, and so far Karen had not led anyone to Christ.

Her main motivation when she enrolled was to help her husband Ken to believe in Jesus. He was not opposed to the Christian faith, and happily attended church on special occasions. However, he had not yet seen the need to make a decision about Jesus Christ for himself. She had presumed, maybe naively as she saw it now, that if she attended a course, he would soon become her first convert. When Ken did not respond, she began to feel despondent and a failure. She concluded that there was obviously a problem with her. She must be a second-class Christian whom God was unable to use. Her morale was at an all-time low.

One particular Sunday Karen was tempted not to go to church, but by lunchtime she was glad that she had. The sermon she heard reminded her of her status and position in Christ. She had been chosen by him; she was one of his privileged people; she belonged to God. Even if her husband had not yet come to Christ, God still loved her deeply. She was not a second-rate Christian at all!

A Prayer Please remind me often, Lord, how special I am to you. Show me that you love me not for what I do, but because I am just 'me'.

A Question to Answer Have you ever sat and meditated for five minutes on how amazing it is that God chose you to be part of his family? Try it! What does this tell you about your value to him?

Listening to God Alone

This poor widow has put in more than all the others (Luke 21:3)

Read: Luke 21:1-4

Beryl tried her hardest to be very discreet about her feelings towards Anna, her friend at church. Actually, Anna was not the problem at all; it was some of the other women who knew them both and made what Beryl considered to be very unfair comparisons. Both Beryl and Anna had husbands who were not Christians, and these other women noticed how often Anna's husband accompanied her to church events while Beryl's husband hardly ever came at all. Beryl always felt that she was perceived as a second-class Christian because her husband was seen at church much less often.

Jesus' comments about the Jewish widow who, of course, had been parted from her husband altogether, showed that the outward appearance does not always reflect the true reality of a situation. In this case, the person who gave the least to the temple treasury actually gave most because it was a far greater proportion of her overall wealth. She probably never knew Jesus was watching her and that he commented to his disciples about her faith, but Jesus wanted his friends to learn an important lesson.

It is so easy for women like Beryl to feel they are overshadowed by others who are apparently better, more spiritual or more successful than them. In reality, this may or may not be the case. What matters is that Beryl, and others like her, keep in close contact with God, seek to follow him faithfully, and cease to worry too much about what other people say. God alone knows how complex these situations are!

A Prayer Help me please, Lord, to listen primarily to you. Protect me from hurtful comments from those who neither know my heart and motives, nor my husband's.

A Practical Suggestion Do not allow yourself to start judging other people if you do not want them to do the same to you!

Seeing Straight

Like a gold ring in a pig's snout is a beautiful woman who shows no discretion
(Proverbs 11:22)

Read: Proverbs 11:16-31

Life at home between Ashley and Kirsty had rarely been easy since they married. Both were fairly volatile, and it was a source of great relief for everyone when Kirsty became a Christian and, almost overnight, began to mellow and become more relaxed. Even this did not prevent some occasional verbal explosions taking place in their home. After these, Kirsty increasingly felt the need to off-load her feelings on to Christian friends whom she knew would understand and support her.

Jane and Belinda, two established Christians, had grown very close to Kirsty since her conversion, and had made it clear that they would always be there to help her when she needed it. After one particularly traumatic session at home Kirsty went to see them, but Ashley followed her and caused a row on the doorstep. He accused her of telling her friends confidential information about their relationship that was no business of theirs.

Once the trauma had died down Kirsty had time to think about what had happened, and she saw things differently. God had given her loyal Christian friends whom she appreciated very much, and whom she knew would do anything to support her. When she has an argument at home though, she does not automatically have the right to betray her husband by criticising him to them. Kirsty realised that while her friends are available for her any time, and this is a wonderful privilege, she needs to use discretion about involving them in the intimate problems in her marriage.

A Prayer Please help me to be careful what I say about my husband to others, even my closest friends. Please give me the self-control I need so that I never betray him unintentionally.

A Practical Suggestion Do not only count to ten before you verbally explode to one of your friends about your husband when he has irritated you. Try to find the time and presence of mind to think through what you will say.

113

Showing God's Love

Pray for those who persecute you (Matthew 5:44)

Read: Matthew 5:43-48

Even Eileen recognised that her situation was unusual. One of her colleagues at work, Jim, was her husband's best friend, and she enjoyed a happy relationship with him as they worked and socialised together. Indeed, there had never been a cross word spoken between them in almost a quarter of a century.

It was when Eileen became a Christian that things began to change. A female colleague at work had become good friends with her, and little by little had told Eileen how much her faith meant to her, and the day came when Eileen placed her own trust in Jesus Christ. However, Jim had taken a dislike to Eileen's friend, and he reported to her husband that he felt she was indoctrinating Eileen. This meant that when Eileen went home and told him about her new faith, he reacted negatively. Not only this, but at work the next morning Jim had a different attitude to Eileen, even at times making sarcastic comments to and about her. What for so long had been a genuinely happy relationship seemed now to be tainted by his disapproval.

Eileen had to decide how to respond. As the words of Jesus' Sermon on the Mount flooded into her mind, she decided not to fight back with sarcasm, nor allow herself to feel hurt or offended so that she became angry. She opted to keep mainly silent. She sensed that Jim had problems understanding God, so if she retaliated it would help no one. She decided to pray hard both for him and her husband.

A Prayer

When it is easier for me to lash out with anger because people misunderstand my faith in you, please help me to meditate on how Jesus responded in similar circumstances.

A Practical Suggestion If you find yourself seething with anger because of some injustice that is either directed at you or someone close to you, find a safe way of releasing it. Your anger is not wrong in itself, but you could do lasting damage if you lash out.

Changing the World

Pray for us (Colossians 4:3)

Read: Colossians 4:2-6

Annie was feeling low the day the postman delivered an airmail letter to her home. That morning she had had a traumatic session with Bernie, her husband. With some trepidation, she had told him she wanted to go to an event at her church one evening later that week. His reaction was as negative as she feared. He accused her of liking the company of her friends at church much more than his, and refused to listen to anything she said in reply. Then he stormed out of the door and went to work.

The contents of Annie's letter helped her to see her own domestic situation more in perspective. Zoe, a friend from church, had emigrated with her husband and family to Australia eighteen months earlier. Both Annie and Zoe had been part of a housegroup that comprised virtually all Christian women whose husbands did not share their faith. Now Zoe was writing to say that her husband had left her to live with his secretary, and to ask Annie and her friends from church to pray. The news shocked Annie, who soon mobilised the prayer support Zoe had asked for.

Paul sent a letter to the church in Colossae asking the Christians there to pray for him. The Apostle knew that physical distance between Christians is no hindrance at all to God. Prayers uttered in one country can affect people radically on the other side of the world. The prayers of Annie and her friends were vital.

A Prayer I want to be faithful in praying for others as well as myself, Lord. As I do, help me to have the faith to believe that you can work powerfully.

A Practical Suggestion Write to or phone someone today who lives out of your own area to encourage them and to find out how you can best pray for them.

Experiencing God's Support

Then the fire of the Lord fell (1 Kings 18:38)

Read: 1 Kings 18:16-39

One Thursday morning Katie was desperate for reassurance that God both understood how she felt and still loved her. She knew that during the previous night she had said some terrible things to Joey when he eventually admitted that he was having an affair with someone at work. Not only was this humiliating for Katie but it was also a huge disappointment. She had been praying for her husband to become a Christian ever since making her own commitment to Jesus three years earlier. Now this seemed more unlikely than ever. Katie was even far from sure that their marriage would survive.

While she knew that she could do with some encouragement from friends, Katie felt that she could not face anyone. She opted to stay at home alone. Joey had gone off to work as usual, the children were at school, and Katie, who had only dozed the night before, slumped into her favourite armchair accompanied by her Bible and a mug of strong coffee. After all the screaming, tears, pain and name-calling of the night before, she wanted to know whether God was still there for her. If he was, she felt that she could just about cope with another day.

Many times during the course of human history, God has burst into people's lives and situations at just the right moment. Elijah experienced this, as did the Psalmist (Ps 30:2). Katie's cry was that God would do the same for her. She needed to know his presence, forgiveness and love, together with some fresh hope and direction for the future.

A Prayer When I feel at my lowest, Lord, please meet me at my point of deepest need. Please give me the reassurance that you will never leave nor forsake me.

A Practical Suggestion Read Psalm 30.

Serving Jesus Faithfully

Lord, even the demons submit to us in your name (Luke 10:17)

Read: Luke 10:1-20

Nothing was going to stop Ruby from rushing round to all the members of her housegroup after church one Sunday. She had some news to tell them before she burst! The people who attended the group were significant because they had specifically prayed for her the previous Wednesday evening when she had arrived rather despondent. Ruby had been a Christian for two years, but felt that her faith had made no noticeable impact on David, her husband. She was desperate for him to become a Christian too.

The housegroup had prayed that Ruby would find a time when she could talk with David and tell him simply and concisely what Jesus had done for her. The right time emerged on Saturday night. With some trepidation lest he ridiculed her, she began to speak. Ruby sensed God's gentle presence and was reassured that her housegroup friends were praying for her. To her amazement, David listened seriously and responded with both interest and respect. He even said that he had noticed a helpful change in some of her attitudes, and to cap it all, he told her again that he loved her.

Ruby was over the moon on Sunday morning. Just as Jesus had sent out his disciples in mission, she felt that he had called her to tell David about her faith. Now that she had, she too had good news to report. True, David was not a Christian yet, but he seemed much closer than he had been!

A Prayer Please give me the courage to tell people I love you, in a simple and concise way.

A Practical Suggestion As it can sometimes be easier to talk seriously with your husband if you go out, try to fix a time in the next few days when the two of you can escape for a couple of hours. Then tell him a little about your faith if God gives you the opportunity, but concentrate on enjoying one another's company.

Trusting a Caring God

Not what I will, but what you will (Mark 14:36)

Read: Mark 14:32-41

Rosanne had had enough. She and Alex were married seven years earlier and had a stormy relationship which often resulted in heated slanging matches. However, the frequency of these had accelerated since she had became a Christian because Alex did not like her going to services and meetings at church. He could be loud and abusive when irritated, and while Rosanne had the capacity to respond in a similar way, she tried hard to honour God by being subdued.

One weekend made her despair. The tension in the house was extreme although Rosanne had little idea as to what had caused it. She could only conclude that it was a build-up of unresolved issues, but during Sunday afternoon she decided that she could tolerate this no more. If marriage provoked such anguish and pain, she would much prefer to be single again.

The next day, as she poured out her heart to a Christian friend, Rosanne had to face a difficult question. Was this what God wanted for her and Alex? She admitted that she had not considered this until then, but promised to do so. Gradually, she realised that the easier option would almost certainly be for her and Alex to separate and prepare ultimately to divorce. The prospect of facing-up to their problems, getting help to work through the areas of contention, and then making changes in their attitudes and behaviour, was not appealing. However, one day Rosanne came to the point where she put the question to God, 'Lord, what do *you* want us to do?'

A Prayer I want to include you in all the major decisions of my life, Lord. Please forgive me when I make independent decisions without asking you first.

A Question to Answer Can you recall in the Bible anyone whose life long-term became more unbearable because they asked for God's guidance and then obeyed it? Christian discipleship is a long-term affair.

Coping with Disappointment

Let us not give us meeting together (Hebrews 10:25)

Read: Hebrews 10:19-25

When they married both Mandy and Craig were committed Christians but, in the years that followed, Craig's relationship with God slowly slipped away. He had to face a number of family traumas, and he became disillusioned with some Christians whom previously he had respected highly. Through all this, Mandy tried to stay close to God, but it was not easy.

Craig stopped attending church when the weather was cold and dull, so while Mandy went he sat happily at home reading the Sunday newspaper. However, when the summer weather arrived, Craig was keen to go out for the day on Sundays and put pressure on Mandy to join him. This put her in an impossible position. She wanted to remain loyal both to God and her husband, and had no desire to feel guilty in the presence of either of them. Not surprisingly, she felt angry sometimes that because Craig had slipped away from God, she now had to choose between them.

As time went on, Mandy realised she was in danger of losing Craig altogether if she was not flexible and co-operative. Her deep conviction was that one day Craig would come back to the Lord. After talking and praying with her pastor, she told Craig that she would miss church every third week to be with him. She hoped dearly that this would be a short-term measure because she felt very uneasy when Sundays passed by and she had not been at church. God's desire for Mandy was her desire too – to meet often with other members of his family.

A Prayer When I face circumstances that make me feel that whatever I do I cannot win, please give me the insight to make wise decisions.

A Question to Answer Are you being flexible enough to handle responsibly the pressures that both God and your husband seem to put before you? Examine any particular areas of tension. What could you do or say to make things easier?

The Identity of Jesus

He is the image of the invisible God (Colossians 1:15)

Read: Colossians 1:15-23

Having studied theology at university, John was not going to allow anyone, including his wife, to suggest that he was unfamiliar with the Bible. However, that was how it came across after Tracey returned home from a church weekend. She had only gone because a friend had invited her, saying it would be fun, but now Tracey seemed passionate about Jesus Christ in a way that John found very hard to grasp.

He had grown-up in a church-going family and from a young age found theology intriguing. At university he studied and evaluated all kinds of religions, but was never tempted to view them as anything more than fodder for academic study and research. Indeed, John could not understand those 'fanatics' who attended church and spoke of God and Jesus Christ in emotive terms. Privately, he despised them and felt that they were wildly misguided. He was not concerned whether there was a God or not, and whether Jesus Christ did or did not exist.

However, John found himself having to confront these issues now that Tracey had come home claiming to have a personal relationship with God. He could not dispute that she seemed genuinely happy and, though excited about her new faith, she seemed controlled, not fanatical. Faced with the evidence of a transformed wife, John began to read the Bible again. Could it really be true that Almighty God existed, and that Jesus Christ came to earth to make him known?

A Prayer Please let my life be a strong witness for you wherever I go, Lord, and especially at home. Help others to see Jesus living in me.

A Practical Suggestion Reflect honestly about your life, and think about any of your actions or attitudes that probably make it harder for other people to believe in Jesus. Repent when you are ready, and ask God to help you to change.

God's Unchanging Desire

God our Saviour…wants all people to be saved (1 Timothy 2:3-4)

Read: 1 Timothy 2:1-7

Recent research gleaned from Christian wives reveals that just 9% of their unbelieving husbands go to church with them. Bert is one who does, although his view is that he is a Christian too. He argues that as he grew up in a Christian family in a Christian country, and as he lives by the Ten Commandments, he has the right to call himself a Christian whatever he believes. Avril, his wife, has tried to explain to him many times that being a Christian is rather more than this, but it has made no difference.

Sparks flew when Bert, certain he was expressing a 'Christian' point of view, argued with Tim, the minister, outside church one Sunday. Tim had preached with conviction about the dire needs of refugees in parts of Africa, and had asked the church to take an extra offering for them. Bert disputed this was a priority, and said that the church should not worry about Africans until it had taken care of homeless people in its own country.

Back home Bert gave Avril a hard time when she openly sided with Tim. The next day over coffee in Tim's study, Avril explained her view of Bert's misunderstanding of Christianity. Tim agreed to visit Bert to continue their discussion, but encouraged Avril to get some close friends together to pray. 'There is no doubt that God loves Bert deeply, but we need to pray that Bert will be open enough to rethink the distortion of Christianity with which he has grown up,' he said.

A Prayer Because you love my husband even more than I do, and want him to be part of your family, please answer my heartfelt prayers for him, Lord.

A Practical Suggestion If your husband is happy to attend church with you, ask him if he will join you at an Alpha course, or some other group which includes a clear presentation of the gospel.

Gaining New Strength

David found strength in the Lord his God (1 Samuel 30:6)

Read: 1 Samuel 30:1-20

Although she certainly was not looking for trouble, Betty found that she and Jack were often at loggerheads. They had been married for over thirty years, their children had grown up and left home, and while they had got on quite well for most of their marriage, Jack had taken exception to Betty becoming a Christian five years before. He had never had any time for religion, and he was appalled when Betty had told him some months afterwards that she had realised God loved her, and she had committed her life to him.

Different things aggravated Jack at different times. Sometimes, because they lived in a small house, he found Betty reading the Bible. He objected to this and always asked her the same thing, 'Why don't you go to the library and get a decent book to read?' He was never happy when she went to church on Sunday mornings, but he tended not to make too much fuss about it because it gave him a couple of hours to potter around quietly in the garden. His biggest hate was meetings related to the church that took her out in the evenings. When she got home she would find him moody and uncommunicative.

Through no fault of his own David found himself unpopular with his men. This was when he looked to God for strength, and was filled again with divine resources. The good news is that in her difficult situation, Betty can do the same.

A Prayer Please give me the sensitivity I need to make wise decisions at home, and strengthen me as I trust in you today. Thank you that your resources will be sufficient whatever I have to face.

A Practical Suggestion Find time today to take a walk so that you can think and pray. As you do, ask God to show you again how rich and powerful his resources are.

Patiently Waiting

Be patient, then, brothers and sisters (James 5:7)

Read: James 5:7-11

Glenda married Darren two years after another couple, who had also met in the local church's youth club, held their wedding. At the time, the wife in the other relationship was a Christian, although her husband was not. However, within eighteen months he too had become a dedicated follower of Jesus Christ. This encouraged Glenda because when she and Darren married he showed only scant interest in her faith. She anticipated that if she prayed a lot and witnessed to him at home, he would soon make a Christian commitment.

However, two years later Darren was no nearer responding to Jesus and Glenda was becoming disillusioned. She felt that he would never be saved and at this stage, of course, no one could be sure. Christian salvation depends not only on God's Holy Spirit working in a person's life, but also on an individual's positive response to the grace of God.

James wrote his New Testament letter to readers who seemed impatient that Jesus had not yet returned as he promised. Little did they know that we would still be waiting! James encourages them to get on with serving the Lord and standing firm for him. Becoming impatient that God has not yet worked as we expected is futile. The best thing Glenda can do is to keep on praying and being a strong witness.

A Prayer Please help me to keep my eyes on you and your strength, Lord, when I might otherwise be tempted to focus on what has not yet happened.

A Practical Suggestion Read one of the psalms that contains exhilarating praise and worship addressed to God.

Not Jumping to Conclusions

Do not judge or you too will be judged (Matthew 7:1)

Read: Matthew 7:1-6

Alison was not sure whether to bite her lip or explode. She was listening to a discussion in her church's housegroup that brought back painful memories of events with which she had not yet fully come to terms. Before she moved and settled in this church, she had been part of a fellowship where she felt she was tried and condemned in her absence.

She had missed Sunday church for a couple of weeks due to family reunions, and other factors had forced her to be away from three housegroup meetings in succession. The next she heard was that some other girls at church had concluded that her commitment, both to God and the church, must be extremely shallow if she attended as irregularly as she did. Alison was relieved that her husband's job had forced them to move a hundred miles north. She felt both angry and hurt at the way she had been misunderstood. God was important to her but, with her husband not being a Christian, she found life was often extremely complicated.

In her new church's housegroup Alison began to feel uptight when the group started to discuss who was missing and why. As they reached the name of another girl who was married to an unbeliever, someone commented on her apparent lack of dedication. Alison erupted inside, and was faced with the dilemma of whether or not to tell the story of her own pain and hurt. Should she speak out or keep quiet?

A Prayer Please help me not to judge others, especially those whose circumstances are virtually unknown to me. Let your love flow from me, as it did from Jesus.

A Question to Answer Have you repented before God, and maybe apologised to the person involved, for the last time when you were judgmental of someone? (Apologies can sometimes make things worse, so think it through first.)

Getting Stronger

The God of all grace...will...make you strong, firm and steadfast
(1 Peter 5:10)

Read: 1 Peter 5:1-11

At times, Lindy wondered if it was all worth it. To run away from everyone and everything seemed an appealing possibility. Home life was tough. Trevor, her husband, had been out of work for four years and increasingly lacked the motivation to chase any jobs he saw advertised. Most days he sat in his armchair in front of the television expecting Lindy to get him food and drink. He resented it when she went out, particularly to church and to meet her Christian friends. He believed that she should be there with him.

As if this was not enough, Lindy had other things to contend with too. Trevor's unemployment meant that they often did not have enough money on which to live comfortably, and therefore the children got very few of the treats that their friends took for granted. Lindy felt bad about this, as she did about the single man at church whom she often sensed was looking at her. That she found him attractive too simply compounded her sense of guilt. It is no wonder that Lindy felt trapped, frustrated and unhappy.

God comes to people like Lindy as they admit to him their weakness and vulnerability. He is able to provide new spiritual strength which can help them to carry on in the face of enormous pressures. Furthermore, he can help them to resist the devil's subtle and appealing temptations. Peter knew from experience that with God's help you can swim instead of sinking.

A Prayer Please help me to entrust any anxiety and pain I have to you. Thank you that whatever is going on in my life, you love me and want to strengthen me so that I can live for you.

A Practical Suggestion Ask your friends to suggest the name of another Christian who has had to cope with serious problems, but who has come through their difficulties stronger with God's help. When they identify someone, try to arrange to talk with that person to gain encouragement.

Taking a Long Time

One who was there had been an invalid for thirty-eight years (John 5:5)

Read: John 5: 1-15

Elsie could not believe how long it had been. She was just a couple of years from retirement and had been a Christian for over thirty years, having been converted soon after she and Ted married. For all this time she had prayed for Ted to become a Christian too, but so far it had not happened. At times she became disillusioned, but on the whole she remained philosophical and kept using special opportunities to invite Ted to church events which would expose him yet again to the gospel.

Ted did not mind this. He knew and understood Christianity sufficiently to know that he was still on the outside. Occasionally he attended baptisms in the church when the people about to be immersed told how their lives had been changed by Jesus Christ, often dramatically. Ted respected what he saw and heard, but at no point did he feel compelled to make any decision for himself. He was not unhappy as he was, although he recognised that some of the Christians he met seemed to have a greater sense of purpose in their lives than he did. Meanwhile, Elsie kept praying.

The man Jesus met at the pool called Bethesda had been unable to walk for thirty-eight years. However, like Elsie, he still hoped that something miraculous would happen one day. His dreams were realised when he met Jesus. Often you have to wait a long time, but then, seemingly out of the blue, Jesus does something dramatic. Elsie should keep on praying...

A Prayer Please encourage me when I find it hard to cope because my prayers have not yet been answered. Help me to keep trusting you however long it takes.

A Question to Answer Do you realise that God often seems to wait before answering our prayers in order to find out how serious we are about what we are asking him?

Scripture Index

5:21-24	37	16:6-10	82	**1 Thessalonians**	
5:35-43	37	16:11-15	75	4:1-12	93
10:46-52	68	18:1-11	55		
13:1-13	90	26:1-32	40	**2 Thessalonians**	
14:32-41	118			3:6-10	30
		Romans			
Luke		15:1-13	91	**1 Timothy**	
1:26-38	50			2:1-7	121
7:1-10	76	**1 Corinthians**		2:8-15	96
7:11-17	67	6:12-20	81		
8:19-21	86	7:1-16	38	**Hebrews**	
10:1-20	117	10:23-11:1	85	10:19-25	119
10:38-42	19	12:1-14	12	11:32-12:3	7
17:11-19	52	16:1-9	105	12:14-29	106
19:1-10	26				
21:1-4	112	**2 Corinthians**		**James**	
		6:14-18	34	3:1-12	41
John		12:1-10	45	5:7-11	123
2:1-11	49				
5:1-15	126	**Galatians**		**1 Peter**	
11:1-44	100	5:13-26	23	1:13-25	74
12:1-8	92			2:4-12	111
14:1-6	32	**Ephesians**		3:1-7	101
20:19-31	103	4:17-27	10	3:8-22	87
		4:29-5:7	14	4:12-19	66
Acts		5:21-6:4	43	5:1-11	125
2:1-16	36	6:5-9	17		
2:14-16	42			**1 John**	
2:36-41	42	**Colossians**		1:5-2:2	57
6:8-15	54	1:15-23	120		
7:51-60	54	2:6-15	25	**Revelation**	
8:26-40	64	3:1-17	15	3:7-13	72
15:36-41	13	4:2-6	115	3:14-22	65